WHERE THE
BUFFALO
ROAM

WHERE THE BUFFALO ROAM

ANNE MATTHEWS

Grove Press
NEW YORK

Published by Grove Press

A division of Grove Press, Inc.

841 Broadway

New York, NY 10003-4793

Published in Canada by General Publishing Company, Ltd.

TOO FAT POLKA by Ross Mac Lean and Arthur Richardson
© 1947 Shapiro, Bernstein & Co., Inc. New York. Renewed.
Used By Permission.

Library of Congress Cataloging-in-Publication Data

Matthews, Anne. 1957–

Where the buffalo roam / by Anne Matthews.—1st ed.

p.   cm.

ISBN 0-8021-1408-3

ISBN 0-8021-3339-8 (pbk.)

1. Wildlife refuges—Great Plains—Planning.   2. Bison, American—
Great Plains.   3. Wildlife reintroduction—Great Plains—Planning.
4. Land use—Great Plains—Planning.   5. Popper, Frank.   6. Popper,
Deborah.   7. Great Plains.   I. Title.

QL84.22.G7M37   1992

333.95'9—dc20   91-33637

CIP

Manufactured in the United States of America

Printed on acid-free paper

Designed by Irving Perkins Associates

Map by Arnold Bombay

First Edition 1992

First Evergreen Edition 1993

1   3   5   7   9   10   8   6   4   2

For CGM and GMM

Acknowledgments

Many people helped this book emerge. My thanks to all those who appear in its pages. Special gratitude goes to Alan Williams, Raymond Anderson, Beth Harrison, Margarett Loke, Lynette Bosch, William Howarth, and the Matthews and Mahoney families (especially Elsie Bronkala Mahoney and Margaret Matthews).

Above all, I wish to thank Frank and Deborah Popper. Without their kindness, enthusiasm, and generosity at every stage, the book would not exist.

Contents

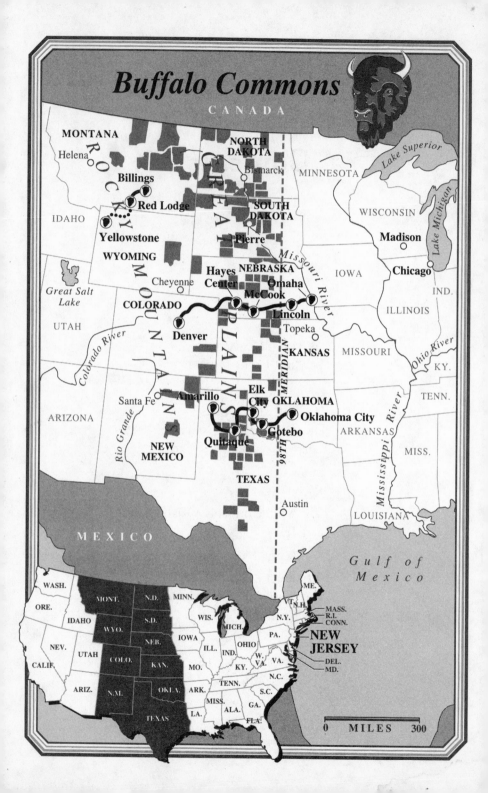

Preface

The Great Plains cover nearly a fifth of America's lower forty-eight states—a big region, with problems to match its size, demanding big ideas. In 1987 an academic couple from suburban New Jersey had the biggest idea ever about the future of the Plains. Driving home one grimy winter afternoon on the New Jersey Turnpike, Frank and Deborah Popper had a sudden, audacious vision for saving the Western prairies.

As experts in American land-use planning and geography, the Poppers realized that much of the Plains is in the process of reverting to frontier conditions only a century after the frontier was declared officially closed. Great stretches of the arid, windswept Great Plains, they argue, are not suited to conventional settlement, and never really were.

Instead, the Poppers would like to see a quarter of the Plains become a massive ecological reserve which they call the Buffalo Commons. As the world's largest natural and historic preservation effort, the Commons would eventually return about 139,000 square miles in ten Plains states to open country for use as a wildlife refuge.

Maybe, the Poppers suggest, the nation can learn from a

hundred years of heartbreak. Maybe we ought not insist on human will over the wishes of the land. Maybe we should yield to history, and bring back the buffalo, and let them roam.

In a pig's eye, say many of the 6.5 million current residents of the Great Plains. Why don't you East Coast professors leave us alone—or else come discuss this face-to-face? This book chronicles a year of the Poppers' journeys on the Plains: a year shaped by the weight of the pioneer past, and by the need of a proud, angry, despairing region of America to choose its future.

To heartland eyes Frank and Deborah Popper can seem like city people, Easterners, outsiders. All those now taking sides in the Buffalo Commons controversy—academics, ranchers, developers, environmentalists, Native Americans, experts in prairie restoration—claim to love the land but passionately disagree on how to treat it. The idealism of a Buffalo Commons exhilarates many people but threatens even more.

Nor is saving our land from ourselves a problem limited to the Great Plains. All over America in the nineties, as urban cores decay, as farmland turns inexorably into malls, as small towns falter, we are anxiously reassessing what it means to have a sense of place and of regional identity, and at what price.

My relatives have lived on the Great Plains and the Midwestern prairies since the 1850s. The terrain of inland America—from southwest Wisconsin's farm valleys to South Dakota's shortgrass range—is the landscape of my earliest memories and deepest affections. I had to go to New Jersey to know how much I owed it. While teaching writing and American literature at Princeton University, I proposed a piece on the Poppers to the *New York Times Magazine*. The editors said yes, and sent me a plane ticket west.

During the journey from that article to this book, I traveled with the Poppers from Montana to Texas, tracking their forays through seminar rooms and small-town living rooms, computer labs, cattle feedlots, and cornfields, watching a turbulent year unfold in the life of an American idea.

I
A BUFFALO
COMMONS

THE GREAT PLAINS

I F YOU WERE TO LOOK at a photograph of the United States
taken from space on a night free of cloud, you would notice
immediately that there *are* no states, nor is there landscape. In
the darkness you see only the continent, three thousand miles of
it, and on this expanse five centuries of settlement history are
inscribed in light. Small towns and cities, metropoli and mega-
burbs ignite the darkness. The nation's lower rim is scalloped by
the glow of Gulf cities, from Galveston to Mobile. West and
East, the great coasts bracket the country in white glare.

But the distribution of this urban brilliance is uneven. The
Eastern Seaboard shines brighter than anything else on the land
mass and is much the hardest population area to read. From
New England down to central Virginia, city spills into city in a
white-water rapids of light. Below the Boston-Washington corridor the crowding eases, but the lights of the antebellum ports
march down the lower Atlantic seaside—Norfolk and Charles-
ton, Savannah and Jacksonville. Florida gleams all around
the peninsula. Atlanta bursts above it like a chrysanthemum
firework.

Moving back up the Appalachian chain, the patches of dark
land begin to widen. The eye counts off the old ways west:
the Cumberland Gap, the Ohio River of flatboats and steam-

boats, the Erie Canal. Along Lake Erie's shore, skeins of light thicken once again, knitting together Pittsburgh and Cleveland, reaching up Huron's western edge to net Detroit. From Gary right around to Milwaukee, the whole lower curve of Lake Michigan is solidly lit.

But beyond Chicago the bright dots that tell where we live begin to drift apart. Across Iowa, across the eastern Dakotas, in eastern Nebraska, the town lights fade and fall away, turning sparse, then sparser still, till the eye reaches the heart of the continent. Here only a scatter of pinpoints shows.

In daylight these cityless lands are revealed as the flat swath of farms and rangeland between the Missouri River and the Rockies' front range. This dry, lightly populated territory covers much of the left half of the nation, but it is not the fashionable West of Boulder or Santa Fe, and never has been. Before the Civil War cartographers believed that this region, and not the Southwest, contained the Great American Desert, and they labeled their maps accordingly. Nowadays dwellers on the coasts are inclined to speak of the same stretch of land, dismissively, as "flyover country."

If you mapped this panorama of the United States at night you would notice that darkness descends like a curtain almost exactly at the 98th meridian, one of the great fault lines of American geopolitics. To geographers the 98th is known as the anhydrous line, past which rainfall turns capricious and farming becomes an art as uncertain as skydiving. To land-use planners these midgrass and shortgrass prairies are the Great Plains, containing two time zones and nearly a fifth the area of the forty-eight contiguous states but barely 3 percent of the American population. To composers of brochures for the region's chambers of commerce and to historians, beyond the 98th is where the West begins, and where the buffalo used to roam.

Two springs ago I bought a *Chicago Tribune* at a newsstand in O'Hare Airport and pushed the paper into my shoulder bag, unopened. The boarding gate for Newark was a concourse away, and I had to run for it. I was on the way home from a wedding in South Dakota, where my cousin from White River (pop. 561) had married a young emergency-room physician from Pierre (pop. 11,973).

Pierre, pronounced "Peeerrr," is South Dakota's capital, and was for years the smallest state capital in America. White River is a one-street prairie town seventy miles south; lively in 1910, progressively less so ever since. White River is the last stop before the Rosebud and Pine Ridge Indian reservations, which are usually counted among the poorest places in America, akin to the Chicago housing projects, the lower Mississippi Delta, or the South Bronx.

Neither my cousin nor her new husband wanted to leave the state of their birth, not really; they liked the somber beauty of the place on its better days, and liked too the odd coziness that still marks the big-area, small-population states of the American West, where nearly everyone you meet either knows you, or knows someone who knows you. But they could not make a life in their childhood towns: there was no work for a doctor and for a high school guidance counselor, no real prospects. After the wedding they would move to Aberdeen, the third largest city in the state (pop. 25,281), which lies on the Great Plains just twenty-five miles west of the 98th meridian.

My cousin is the only one of my generation to stay in the

region. Our grandfather was born in 1890, the year of the ghost dances all across the Plains, the year of the winter massacre of Sioux by the Seventh Cavalry at Wounded Knee, the last formal military encounter between the United States and Indian tribes. Our grandfather's family had left the gentle lake country of Ontario for Dakota ranching adventure and regretted it ever after. Our grandmother grew up in a sod house west of Pierre; like her mother before her she taught in a one-room prairie schoolhouse before she was seventeen. Of their five children, raised in Pierre during Dust Bowl, Depression, and war, two live today on the Plains. Of eight grandchildren, only the one remains. All the others left long since, scattering to Denver, Chicago, Minneapolis, Ohio, New Jersey.

But nearly everyone came back for the wedding, complaining how hard it is to get to Pierre anymore. In the 1940s the state capital rated two passenger trains a day east, two west; in 1992 none arrive or depart. Amtrak stops nowhere in South Dakota. In the 1960s the town was connected to the world outside the Plains by propjets, bouncy DC-3s with plush seats that faced each other, making the milk run from Watertown to Aberdeen to Pierre to Rapid City and the Black Hills and back again.

"Have a nice day," the flight attendants would say as they loosed you into Pierre's dust storms or blizzards, adding, realistically, "—if you can."

The 1970s were best. The Plains got rain then; not much, but enough to let people tell themselves times were improving, after a hundred years of repeated disappointments. Pierre acquired a King's Inn motel, a mall, a restaurant with heavy linen napkins and Boston lettuce in the salads. In the seventies, you went to Pierre on the Rancher's Special, a packed 737 that sometimes made an illegal but entertaining circle over Hughes County and the Missouri River before landing to let passengers admire the Oahe Dam and Reservoir.

The Oahe complex is one of the great postwar feats of the Army Corps of Engineers. Planned by the 1944 passage of the Pick-Sloan public works agreement and finished in 1963, the Oahe Dam is the largest on the Plains. Its pent-up waters, when released, regulate river levels and meet irrigation and power demands from the Dakotas all the way to St. Louis. In late spring and early summer the country east of the river and the reservoir is usually green, or trying to be. West of the river the dry rangelands begin, tan and sienna and fawn, tenanted by Herefords and rattlesnakes and the world's largest private buffalo herd, the one rented out for the movie *Dances With Wolves*.

In the 1990s the amenities are dwindling. Pierre has no jet service at all anymore, and no Greyhound, though the Jackrabbit Lines bus stops at the filling station on Sioux Avenue. Most people get to Pierre by car on two-lane roads unwidened since Model T days. U.S. 90, the interstate, lies forty miles south, on the other side of the Brule and Crow Creek Indian reservations.

I came to my cousin's wedding, or tried to, in a nineteen-seat commuter plane with an army blanket slung between cabin and cockpit, and landing gear that refused to lower. While the pilot pondered whether to take his chances in Pierre or go on to Rapid City, where the runway could be foamed, I grew uneasy watching fire engines, each with its crash team in protective gear, assemble at the airport's edge. As the small plane labored up and down and up the Missouri I watched instead the glittering Oahe Reservoir advance and recede under the wing, a life-giving blue in the dun landscape.

Around the reservoir's edges I saw something that was not supposed to be there. Drying lakebed rimmed the basin on every

7

side, and the docks and bait shops and marinas built in the heady seventies for a projected vast recreation and fishing trade stood marooned in a quarter-mile of mud flats. Beset by three years of Plains-wide drought, the invincible Oahe, ordinarily a mile wide and 230 miles long, was visibly shrinking. Between 1986 and 1990 the reservoir's water levels had receded twenty-eight feet.

We came in over the Hughes County airfield for a tipping, roaring landing. The two-man crew flung themselves from the cockpit doors almost before the propellers stopped turning, and ran. The passengers stoically improvised an evacuation—a rancher read the instructions on the exit, a Sioux housewife collected the pillows we had clutched over our heads—and three hours later I sat in the thin shade of a cottonwood in a sunny Pierre backyard, eating three-bean salad and brownies and listening to angry talk.

Many of the wedding guests were upset about a pair of wacko professors from New Jersey, a husband-and-wife team claiming that large parts of the Plains were doomed, that the best move might be to bring the buffalo back, that prairie land wasn't meant for much else, that settling this country at all had been a terrible mistake.

"By God," said my uncle Thomas, "we won't let them turn Aberdeen into a buffalo pasture." For forty years Tommy has taught grade school and high school music in White River, drilling ranchers' kids and adolescent Sioux in Bach and Basie, driving his students eight and twelve hours in elderly buses to music contests, so that when they marry at fifteen or sixteen, as often happens, they will have something wonderful to remember.

He has spent his life, he sometimes thinks, riding the Plains in buses full of instrument cases. When Tommy was fifteen, in

1940, he was offered a weekend job playing tenor saxophone for Johnny Big Eagle and the Red Ramblers. The Ramblers were one of the first integrated bands on the Plains (integrated in that time and place meaning Indian-white) and thus a great social novelty. "How horrid!" said my grandmother when she heard—she had little tolerance for the big-band sound and not much more for Indians—but it was a big chance for a boy from Pierre, and she let him go.

All through the 1940s and 1950s Tommy was on the road, doubling on trombone and sax with a dozen of the traveling swing bands, called territory bands, that packed dances from Deadwood to Minot. A good territory band could play creditable swing and blues, improvising as freely as any big-city jazz group, then turn right around and honor the inevitable polka requests from farmers with water-slicked hair and pressed blue jeans ("Play the 'Too Fat Polka'! 'I don't want her, you can have her/She's too fat for me' ").

The crowds always turned out though, two, three, four hundred at a time. People drove in from ranches and farms and little towns, looking for Saturday-night respite from a life of toughing it out. "Toughing it out" has been the Great Plains motto for generations, an abiding conviction that supernal grit equals true virtue. A hard life keeps the riffraff out. If you don't like it here, leave.

Tommy at sixty-six is still on the road, two weekends out of four. He just recruited a fine tenor sax man from Rapid City, a Sioux named Freddy Whiteface, and the Tommy Matthews Band has never sounded better. In Iowa, in Minnesota, in eastern Nebraska, the crowds still come out to hear them, and it is almost like the old days, but the small Dakota towns that Tommy has played all his life trouble him. Two dozen couples may turn up. Or only a dozen. Sometimes not even that.

9

"And the rest aren't home watching pro basketball on cable, either," he told me. "There's less than seven hundred thousand people in this state in a good year. Outside the big towns, the place is just emptying out." Many of those who still make it to school gyms and Legion halls to hear him are too old to polka now, certainly too old to lindy. On the Plains there are more old people than anywhere else in America except Florida, and fewer young families.

At 31,000 feet over Harrisburg, Pennsylvania, I finally paged through the Chicago paper. Tucked in beside the Board of Trade farm prices (wheat down, hogs lower, soybeans steady) was a brief Associated Press item, datelined Bismarck, North Dakota. Its headline announced:

Rutgers Couple Get An Earful On The Plains.

Two New Jersey scholars who predict the Great Plains will revert back to the days when it was home for buffalo got discouraging words from the human herd that lives there now.

The pair faced hostile questions from 125 North Dakota journalists and others, but Frank Popper and Deborah Epstein Popper say the heated reaction from area residents—one called their work "Popperscock"—is tinged with fear that their theory of an emptying Plains is prophetic.

"What the hell do you want us to do about it? Leave?" said Mark Carlson, editor of the weekly *Pierce County Tribune.*

"I hope they enjoy it back home in toxic Jersey," said Lauren Donovan of the weekly *Hazen Star.* "Such foolishness could only have come from a place like that."

But Ellen Swendsen of western North Dakota said the couple's views are not unrealistic. "The challenge has been laid square in our lap," she said. "I walk around and count the empty houses and shudder."

I decided to give the Poppers a call. Rutgers is in New Brunswick, New Jersey; I live in Princeton, half an hour down the road. As they say on the Plains, it seemed only neighborly.

Frank and Deborah Popper and I are gazing out from the flat rooftop of Lucy Stone Hall, a three-story classroom building at Rutgers University. On a warm and windy weekday, with summer coming on, the afternoon sky is robin's-egg blue, paling to a soft pollution haze of yellow-gray and pearl all around the horizon—central Jersey at its most beguiling. We kick idly at the tarred pebbles underfoot, not wanting to go back indoors.

Frank Popper, an urban and regional planner, is forty-six years old. He chairs the Department of Urban Studies at Rutgers. Deborah Epstein Popper, forty-two, is a geographer, teaching at the university and working on her Ph.D. We crane our necks, then stand on tiptoe, trying to see past a throng of gray cement dormitory towers, trying for an uninterrupted view westward. We are looking for the Great Plains.

"Out there!" declares Frank Popper, flinging his arm in the direction of Tallahassee. Deborah Popper gently redirects his index finger toward the low green Watchung hills that rise beyond the campus edge.

"Thataway," she suggests.

"Fine," says her husband. "Whatever. Want to see me locate the World Trade Center?"

On this assignment, he does better. Crouching among the air vents by the building's parapet, peering east, we can just make out the tallest buildings at Manhattan's tip. In the seventeenth century, Henry Hudson sailed his caravel past that island's west side and up a broad river thronged with seven-foot sturgeon, scanning the palisaded cliffs as he went, hoping to find a convenient passage to the Pacific. At Manhattan's far north end perhaps twenty of the wooded acres glimpsed from Hudson's quarterdeck remain undeveloped from that day to this—a tiny bit of original green. All the rest have disappeared under three hundred years of urban and regional planning decisions and indecisions.

The Poppers spend their days thinking about geography, planning, and the future of the Great Plains while living at the core of the highest-density area in the United States, breathing some of America's most heavily industrialized air. From our rooftop aerie, beyond a colony of warehouses, we spot first a scatter of strip development, then the great power-transmission towers lining Route 1. In this part of New Jersey the highway noise never stops, nor does the roar and whistle of commuter trains and Metroliners pounding down the New York–Washington rail corridor nearby, nor the whine overhead of planes on final approach to Newark Airport. Looking down instead of out, we glimpse the university parking lot, yellowing pines and a strip of dying lawn, then more asphalt and concrete.

"Environmental 'ring around the collar,' " says Frank Popper glumly, when I ask him to tell me what he sees. "An alienating landscape, cynical, corrupt, despairing. You can drive for miles here and never see a human being, only cars and warehouses. Jersey development turns my stomach, but these infinite interlocked characterless webs seem to be the future. It depresses me enormously." He paces the roof, rubbing his glasses on his raveling navy sweater.

"We are creating an uglier and uglier place here, which makes those who inhabit it angrier and angrier. I'm interested in the American West because change still feels possible there, unlike

the bleak and difficult East. The Plains can be bleak and difficult too, but not like this hopeless . . ." His gesture takes in
Greater New York. His round face creases unhappily.

"Most of this is classified by the zoning boards as semirural,
can you believe it?" We turn away to climb through a trapdoor
and down an iron ladder, Frank hurrying, two rungs at a time,
Deborah's footholds neat and quick.

Along the long hallway that forms the domain of the Rutgers
Department of Urban Studies, many of the faculty-office doors,
as is the custom in academe, are exercises in whimsical self-
expression. *New Yorker* cartoons are heavy favorites; so are cal-
ligraphed ads for East Coast livestock ("Attention! We are leaving
for Palo Alto and need a home for our wonderful cat Grendel.
He is kind and friendly, sleeps much, eats little, and does impres-
sions").

But the department chair's door is a dense montage of postcards from Plains states, nearly all featuring cloudless skies and
golden grain. The interior of Frank Popper's office is full of
buffalo. Buffalo thunder across posters on the pale-blue cin-
derblock walls, glower from coffee mugs, pose gracefully on
tacked-up bumper stickers. On the filing cabinet, atop a battered
atlas, stands a paper sack of dried buffalo droppings.

"Genuine Virgin Buffalo Chips," the label reads. "Permeate
Your Patio with the Pungency of the Old West's Pioneer Fertilizer
and Fuel. Not for Microwave Ovens. Contents Public Domain."

Frank and Deborah Popper would like to return much of the
Great Plains to its primeval condition, buffalo herds and all.
Over the next forty years, the Poppers argue, depressed and
underpopulated portions of ten Plains states should become a
massive ecological reserve, incorporating, they estimate, about

139,000 square miles of open land and wildlife refuge. On a wall map of current federal lands, Frank points out the projected reserve areas. The affected zone includes much of the western Dakotas, western Nebraska, and eastern Montana; sizable portions of Kansas, Oklahoma, and Texas; and bits of Colorado, New Mexico, and Wyoming. In all, 110 counties, or a quarter of the Great Plains, are sufficiently distressed to warrant inclusion in the Poppers' research. These areas contain about 413,000 of the 6.5 million current residents of the Plains.

The Poppers call their vision the Buffalo Commons. Set in place, it would become the world's largest natural and historic preservation project, a massive act of ecological restoration that boldly reverses three centuries of American settlement and land-use history. Visitors to such a Commons would see the heart of the continent as Lewis and Clark first knew it: hundreds of miles of windswept grass and migrant game.

For Indians and for the early cattlemen, the entire Plains area was originally a commons. Animals and people constantly migrated across it, to graze and camp and then move on, allowing a dry and fragile ecosystem to renew itself. The nineteenth century's determination to conquer and transform the Plains put the native prairies to the plow, grew towns overnight where buffalo wallows used to be, launched a thousand Hollywood sodbuster sagas, and set in motion an intensely extractive economy. The Poppers' research suggests that the epic struggle to tame the Plains, and to mine it of topsoil and oil and gas and water, has also been the largest, longest-running environmental (miscalculation) in the nation's history.

In its place the Poppers offer a flurry of what-ifs. What if a younger America had accepted that the Plains are not arable

14

country, at least not as understood in the green lands east of the 98th meridian? What if we had not tried to force arid Oklahoma to behave like rich-earthed Ohio, piling on the pesticides and the herbicides, the sodbusting and the rip-up harvesting? The classic Plains boom-and-bust cycle of drought, financial woe, and depopulation is rolling again; what if this time it goes all the way? Frank Popper has been pacing his office, brooding aloud. Now he sighs.

"The history of the American West is largely the chronicle of one long continuous hopeful feverish real-estate transaction, and a lot of people, mostly those who could least afford it, got burned."

But the Plains, splendid and sparsely settled, may hold a number of other possibilities. Imagining them is the land-use specialist's craft. Describing the conditions that create them is the geographer's art. Frank Popper leans back in his swivel chair and stretches, then runs over some of the alternatives.

The Plains are the bulk of the Louisiana Purchase. Was the region intended from the first as a land reserve, a national nest egg? Thomas Jefferson seems to have acquired the continent's grasslands in precisely this spirit, believing that though his contemporaries might not know what to do with such lands, their descendants likely would.

Or are the Plains a real-estate white elephant of unprecedented scale despite a century and a half of public and private investment? Wells dry, mortgages unmet, might millions of eroded and degraded acres drop into the taxpayers' lap in another generation, the S & L of American land use? Conventional economic reckonings go haywire at the 98th. No one, on the Plains or off, bureaucrat or academic, developer or environmentalist, holds exactly the same vision of the region's future or its fiscal health. Charges and countercharges have piled up for decades, like tumbleweeds against a barbed-wire fence.

Some facts no one disputes. The Plains are rural, but they are no longer overwhelmingly agricultural. On the Northern Plains, drought and population loss are emptying Montana's flat eastern three-quarters. North Dakota is a state in trouble, its farmland dropping 40 percent in value in twenty years, its population smaller now than in 1930. (In North Dakota in the 1980s, three of four new jobs were non-farm, and more yet were outside the state's Plains areas. In the same decade, North Dakota's population fell by 10 percent—again, a loss concentrated in the western, or Plains, section of the state.)

South Dakota must contend with population leakage too, plus racial tensions. The Great Plains have the most homogenous overall population of any American region—95 percent white—but South Dakota's eighty thousand Native Americans remain a largely unassimilated presence a century after the tragedy at Wounded Knee.

The Central Plains (western Nebraska, western Kansas, and Colorado's dry eastern expanses) present a somewhat less daunting economic picture but worry even more about water. Western Kansas has less than fifty years' irrigation supply in its portion of the underground Ogallala aquifer. More water-rights lawyers practice in Colorado than in any other U.S. state. And on the Southern Plains, Oklahoma and Texas face sobering aquifer problems and population loss, as their mixed economies of minerals extraction and agriculture boom and falter.

If the backcountry and small-town Plains are emptying out and the great natural aquifers and elegantly engineered reservoirs are drying up, does this mean the American frontier is somehow reemerging? The Census Bureau declared the American frontier closed in 1890, when few large areas of blank space remained on maps of the nation to indicate unsettled land. Now, the Poppers suggest, the blank spaces seem to be returning, even expanding. What should we do about it? What did the Plains look like, anyway, before 1890, before 1870, before 1850, before white settlement? What if we were to try to find our way back to the America that might have been?

"We are pursuing *scholarship*, not advocacy," says Deborah Popper firmly. Fine-boned and dark-haired, she is sitting across the sunny office, labeling a pile of computer disks, listening to her husband think aloud. "Consider the Buffalo Commons as a metaphor, if you like. Ours is not a knee-jerk environmentalist approach. We just want to get people talking about the future of a region."

Not all the talk is friendly. "We wanted to stimulate public debate," mourns Deborah, "not turn into public figures ourselves. Even here, when I take our son Nicholas to swim meets and introduce myself, I get jokes, or second looks. 'Oh, the *controversial* Popper,' the other parents say."

The Buffalo Commons proposal evokes double takes west of the Missouri too; also denial, dismissal, tears, rage, and name-calling. The Park Service has made nervous inquiries about the pair's early use of the term "national park." City managers in Nebraska call them ("from public phone booths, after dark," says Frank) to bemoan the implications of Popper data for local bond issues.

Politicians up and down the Plains, scenting reelection, have leaped to denounce the Buffalo Commons and its inventors. The Poppers have been publicly criticized by two U.S. secretaries of agriculture, four Plains senators, and every Plains state chief executive (governors Sinner of North Dakota, Janklow of

South Dakota, Bellmon of Oklahoma, and Romer of Colorado being the loudest protestors).

Says Governor Mike Hayden of Kansas, tartly, "America's Great Plains do not equal the Sahara. Why not seal off declining urban areas while we're at it, and preserve them as museums of twentieth-century architecture?" Pat Roberts, a U.S. representative from Kansas, complained in the *Washington Post*, "At best, the Popper plan is elitist and condescending. The end result would be famine and economic devastation. The nation's breadbasket would welcome a visit from the professors any time they care to leave their ivory tower in New Jersey to see for themselves the irreplaceable contributions of these states." Bob Dole's press secretary has suggested putting the Poppers in front of a buffalo stampede. The flap has made the couple as recognizable as rock stars in Great Plains states, at least by name.

"I understand a survey last year showed that we score higher recognition ratings on the Plains than some sitting governors," says Frank with lugubrious satisfaction.

Frank Popper begins to sort his morning mail. His notion of sorting is to toss items onto towering paper piles that sprawl along the office walls and on his desk. From these he is able to retrieve any document requested, pausing like a dowser, then plunging his hand into the appropriate stack.

A former Cabinet member has sent a letter of praise for a recent journal article on land reform. Speaking invitations to Gdansk and Toronto turn up. So does an essay from a student in his seminar on American Land, packaged in a bright red binder to atone for lateness. Then a four-page form on interdepartmental transfer-credit options, to be returned to the dean's office *at once*. In a plain brown envelope, a scrawled missive:

Dear Professor Popper,
So, what state did you write off *this* morning?
Sincerely,
Citizens for a Better South Dakota

Frank Popper recognizes the handwriting (a Rutgers graduate student given to planners' humor) but tapes the letter to
his office door anyway. To get it there he must stretch over his
most imposing piles, the genuine mail received to date
on the Buffalo Commons. The postmarks on these letters
are from towns like Hamilton, Montana (pop. 2,661); Wal-
halla, North Dakota (pop. 1,429); and Fredonia, Texas (pop.
50). Some of his correspondents are temperate, others enraged.
Frank cannot resist a good letter, or even a bad one. Typing
four-fingered on a Vietnam-era Royal electric, he will answer
them all.

One corridor west, Deborah Popper sits in a windowless
room, sandaled feet wrapped around the legs of a metal chair,
typing steadily on a computer keyboard. She pauses frequently
to consult a fat volume of Census Bureau tables. Twelve battered
Proteus computers crowd the tabletops around her. Their wide
color monitors are busy drawing maps of Montana and Kansas,
forming each image county by county, then labeling all counties
by name.

Montana's names offer a geographical poetry: Deer Lodge,
Sweet Grass, Silver Bow, Musselshell. Kansas favors surnames
of settlers and military men (Osborn, Graham, Ellis, Stanton,
Riley, Meade). It seems deceptively sober nomenclature for a
state thought to be the height of frontier exoticism by young
Easterners in the 1870s, imaginations fed by Currier and Ives
prints of gory scalpings and dime novels with Kansas settings and

titles like *Among the Pawnees; or, Jack the Daring Buffalo-Hunter.*

In a week the Poppers will be out traveling on the Central Plains. Their speaking itinerary begins in southwestern Nebraska, near the Kansas border. Deborah taps a command, and Nebraska's counties appear on the screen before us, forming a constellation of strong clear names—Box Butte and Antelope, Red Willow and Hayes.

Another sequence of keys, and indicators of economic and social distress for the state of Nebraska begin to combine. Like the other nine Plains states, Nebraska is one political unit with several ecologies and several economies. On Deborah's computers, parts of eastern Nebraska (a land of oats, corn, soybeans, large cities, and comparatively high rainfall) would register as healthy and prosperous. But much of western Nebraska (cattle and sheep and wheat country entering a third year of drought) fills swiftly with the red crosshatch lines that mark areas vulnerable to decline.

"Oh, my, not encouraging," she says, chin propped on hand, forefinger moving over the curved glass of the Proteus monitor.

County by county, Deborah has built statistical portraits of land-use distress for the Plains states. One indicator is population loss from 1930 to 1988. Whereas many counties in the Dakotas have lost half or more of their population in that period, parts of western Nebraska seem to be holding their own, especially in the towns on or near the Platte River and Interstate 80, though Deborah's programs immediately flag danger zones like Hayes County (pop. 1,356).

Population loss of 10 percent or more between 1980 and 1988 is another warning sign of land-use distress. So are low-density counties, with four or fewer people per square mile (the U.S.

average being 68.1), and counties with a median age of thirty-five or higher (the U.S. median is thirty years). A poverty rate of 20 percent or more among a county's residents (U.S. rate: 13.5 percent) is yet another key, as is new-construction investment of $50 or less per capita (U.S. average: $850). As an additional index of economic health, Deborah incorporates each county's Dun and Bradstreet ratings. Environmental data, like soil erosion and irrigation rates, are not comparable by county and must be reconstructed and factored in using reports from state geologists' offices.

Deborah works principally from U.S. Census Bureau statistics, considered by geographers the most detailed and uniform. In Deborah's case the decision to use federal statistical packages has meant much extracting and reentering of data, since the census districts do not follow America's bioregions, as the Poppers are trying to do.

In juxtaposing geographical, economic, and demographic data, Deborah is also attempting to map the secrets of survival and stability. Why are some small Plains towns dying while others are clearly possessed, against long odds, of the will to live? She wants to isolate what factors make the difference. Yet if she succeeds in finding even partial answers, the practical and philosophical questions only multiply. Can the emptying of a region be stopped? Should it be?

She types in more commands. The computer map shifts again, to show the entire Great Plains. From the 98th meridian to the Rockies, scarlet indicators of land-use distress stain the screen, growing and spilling across ten states.

Frank and Deborah Popper live a mile from the Rutgers campus, on a sycamore-shaded street in Highland Park, New

Jersey (pop. 13,396), which is part of the New Brunswick–Edison–Perth Amboy–Sayreville metroweb (pop. 595,893). By car, New York is forty-five minutes northeast, Philadelphia two hours southwest. The view from the front porch of the Poppers' turn-of-the-century frame house is a synopsis of mixed-use urban development: single-family homes, gas station, turnpike employees' union hall, tire shop, and K-9 Dog Grooming Service.

The Popper house is full of books and scholarly apparatus, some still sitting in unpacked boxes in the hallways. Like many of their peers on the academic and public-policy circuits, Frank and Deborah have been nomads for most of a twenty-three-year marriage. They have moved from a New York foundation (the Twentieth Century Fund) to Chicago consulting operations (Public Administration Service, the American Society of Planning Officials) to Washington, D.C., research institutes (the Environmental Law Institute, Resources for the Future) and, in 1983, to Frank's first university appointment, at Rutgers, the state university of New Jersey.

For people who want to reorder a continent, the Poppers live in some disarray. Plates and muffins and orange-juice cartons are wedged among computer printouts when I join them for breakfast a day after our rooftop excursion. Their mealtime talk, conducted at table-tennis speed, is of TOADS and LULUs. The former are Temporarily Obsolete Abandoned Derelict Sites (the overgrown lots, abandoned houses, or empty manufacturing plants which signal the bottom of a land-use cycle). LULUs are Locally Unwanted Land Uses, or pariah development projects: Frank's pet scholarly invention before the Plains and its problems lured him away.

"If I'd kept the intellectual pedal to the floor," he announces, looking for the strawberry preserves, "LULU rather than NIMBY (i.e., Not In My Backyard) could be America's acronym of choice for landfills, nuclear waste dumps, and the like. So near, and yet so far."

The jam jar is sitting on a review copy of *Zoning and the American Dream* at the other end of the table, where Deborah and their seventeen-year-old daughter are looking through more paper piles, trying to find Joanna's physics homework. Joanna is also lobbying her mother for permission to put Grateful Dead stickers on the family car, a request artfully timed, since Deborah is distracted by twelve-year-old Nicholas's soccer-practice schedule. Deborah is off carpool duty this night, but on the next.

"Can't you get your friends to wash their socks? I had to drive with the windows open last time," she says to her son, who swallows a pint of milk in one long, steady gurgle and unfolds from his chair.

"Coach says smelly feet intimidate the opposition, really psychs them out," he tells her patiently. Frank, passing by with a third cheese Danish in hand, traps Nicholas in an affectionate headlock and they vanish out the front door into the gray New Jersey morning. The wind is from the north today. To Deborah and me, still at the breakfast table, it brings into the house a hum of traffic from heavily traveled Route 27, a half-block away, and the acrid smell of the Exxon Bayway Refinery, twenty miles to the north.

The Buffalo Commons idea came to the Poppers beside the Bayway in the spring of 1987. On the way home from a geographers' conference, stuck in twelve-lane traffic on the New Jersey Turnpike, they began to argue ("to *discuss*," amends Deborah) the many insolubles and paradoxes, historical, social, and ecological, of the Great Plains.

"Oh, just turn it back to the buffalo, let *them* have it!" said Deborah finally, exasperated.

"A buffalo homeland," said Frank.

"A Buffalo Commons," they said together, as traffic slowed to a crawl in the urban badlands near where the Jersey meadowlands disappear completely under asphalt, close to the Verrazano Bridge exit for Staten Island.

The Poppers' choice of the word "commons" to describe a possible future for the Great Plains stems from renewed international interest, among economists, governments, and land-use planners, in the cooperative management of natural resources, from rainforests to fishing grounds. Settling the American prairies, the Poppers often argue, was a classic case of what the ecologist Garrett Hardin has called the "tragedy of the commons"—plausible private incentives eventually leading to disastrous public consequences, when common land is overexploited without regard for the ability of resources like water and soil to renew themselves, and without regard for fitness of supply.

In the United States the idea of commons is a rediscovery, not an innovation: the Boston Common is headed for its third century. As recently as the 1970s, American land-use specialists regarded the commons as an essentially archaic tradition, lost with the felling of Eastern forests and the fencing of the Plains. In the 1980s, with the spread of UNESCO's program to protect crucial ecologies through a system of voluntary biosphere reserves, the venerable commons idea revived, promising a balance of the claims of development and of bio-heritage.

In the winter of 1987 the Poppers wrote a fifteen-page essay on the future of the Plains ("The Great Plains: From Dust to Dust") that appeared in *Planning*, the more reader-friendly of the two principal publications in the urban and regional planning field. Both Poppers assumed that their prescription of a Buffalo Commons for the struggling Plains was destined, like most academic work, for oblivion. Frank's previous four books and forty-nine scholarly articles had provoked a total of eleven letters to journal editors.

Then *Planning* called them, elated; the piece had drawn a record response, some readers hailing the Poppers' work as brilliant and original; others (mostly from zip codes west of the Missouri River) suggesting just as urgently that the pair be strung from the nearest available cottonwood.

Plains newspapers and radio stations began to announce and denounce the Poppers' theory. An alert staffer in the office of North Dakota governor George Sinner spotted and circulated the *Planning* piece. Throughout 1988, as drought killed crops and dried fields across the Plains, Governor Sinner's speeches pointedly disparaged Eastern academic arrogance.

Editorial pages weighed in, also sounding less than grateful. (The Aberdeen, South Dakota, *American News*: "New Jersey ethnocentrism . . . Leave us alone!" The Mandan, North Dakota, *News*: "The Poppers cannot comprehend what we love about this wide-open and windy space, and you can't explain it to them. Droughts, blizzards, grasshoppers and hail either drive you from this land or bind you unbreakably to it." A columnist in Wichita, Kansas: "Let's turn New Jersey into a Dumping Commons, the permanent home of anything America wants rid of . . . nuclear waste, garbage, Jimmy Hoffa's body.")

Mail by the sackful began arriving at Lucy Stone Hall. One letter was addressed only to The Buffalo People, Urban Studies, Crackpot Division, Noisome Jersey. Thundering Herd Buffalo Products, of Reno, Nevada, sent a catalogue. An eighth-grade class in rural Kansas wrote to say they now observed a weekly

Popper Day, dedicated to the study of Plains history and ecosystems. An urgent funding plea came from the Center for Rural Affairs in Walthill, Nebraska (pop. 900):

> Dear Friend,
> Did you see recently where a couple of professors from the East made the news with a proposal to empty the farms and towns on the Great Plains and turn the whole place into a national park—a Buffalo Commons? Help us scold the professors and defend the region! Send your annual donation today!

Frank and Deborah dutifully sent a check for their own eradication.

The overwhelming initial wave of response to the Buffalo Commons proposal quickly forced the Poppers onto levels of intellectual accountability usually reserved for the hardest of hard sciences. Their *Planning* piece, conceived in an industrial wilderness, was heavy on description, prophecy, and the poetry of place. The resulting torrent of practical worries from mayors and ranchers and wildlife managers and agribusiness companies served as counterweight, valuable because unexpected.

What might be the price tag on a Buffalo Commons? ("Billions," says Frank, "but still far less than current farm subsidies to grow crops already in surplus.") On a Buffalo Commons would the Poppers allow military bases? (Yes.) Oil derricks? (Yes.) Hazardous waste dumps, or hazardous waste exported from Eastern states? ("Certainly not," says Frank. Deborah disagrees. "It's not for us to decide," she says.) What about predators for buffalo, such as mountain lions and prairie wolves? (Yes.) Indians? (Definitely.) As the Poppers thought out each reply the once-nebulous Commons acquired clarity and heft.

"Like writing a novel," says Frank, who once wanted to. "But what we never counted on was the way the image of returning buffalo appears to touch on some primal apocalyptic terror, or else some equally primal sense of Edenic rightness, depending on the listener."

They made some memorable mistakes. They found they had underestimated the economic importance of the Plains' spring wheat crop—a tactical error that gratified the spring-wheat-growing states, especially North Dakota. But even with more accurate wheat figures added, Popper projections for the region's grim future stayed grim.

Neither Popper has had much experience with the rural. Deborah spent summers in Massachusetts as a child and remembers friendly cows and waist-high ferns and blueberry picking. She never saw the West until 1971. Frank waxes grandiloquent, when cornered, about his boyhood on the prairies of Illinois, by which he really means the park next to his family's Chicago apartment building near the top of Lake Shore Drive, six miles north of the Loop. Frank began to travel the Plains in the 1970s as a federal land-use consultant, negotiating tribal grant applications and calming water-rights quarrels. The more he saw of the region, the more he began to wonder why the lands west of the 98th lived in such defiance of nature and were so ruled by the dead hand of the past.

Deborah had already evidenced a nose for land controversy with her Rutgers master's thesis in geography, on the audacious (and successful) million-acre land claims put forth in the 1970s by Maine's Passamaquoddy and Penobscot tribes. Place-loyalty plus major money, she learned in the Maine woods, can be volatile in the extreme, and can yield instructive cultural geography. The Poppers started talking, over meals and on the way to school, about the Plains as an even more complex set of entrenched interests which, as perceptive aliens, they might investigate.

Frank swings loafered feet onto his crowded desktop. "Our collaboration is instinctive, irrational, and I guess not very academic, at least not in the three-footnote, five-regression-analysis social science tradition," he says. Frank will flip to the back of a mystery to see who did the murder, Deborah won't. He starts arguments, she backs them with data. He sees the patterns, she traces connections. He galvanizes her, she steadies him. Frank writes the drafts of their articles on the Plains and on the future of the American frontier. Deborah edits, rewrites, rearranges, replaces flash with substance. The margins of their working drafts quickly fill with emendation and counter-emendation in red and blue pen: "Sequence is off," "Why do we say this?" "What about aquifer loss?" And, when Deborah becomes exasperated, "Enough of your witticisms!"

For all his pleasure in the platform ("Deborah is the demon for fact in this family. There's a lot of Elvis in me, and entertainment values in the academy are pretty low"), Frank at extended-family gatherings will retreat to the living room and steadfastly read the day through, till everyone else has gone to bed and he can breathe again.

"I know full well I'm a moody, eccentric dork," he says, jumping up to frown at, then sign, an undergraduate's course card. At that remark the student throws his professor a nervous glance and ducks back out the door. Deborah is much less comfortable before crowds but better with them, practicing one-on-one politicking and persuasion.

"If Frank had been a pioneer," she says with ironic affection, handing him a fresh pile of letters, "he would have died before he got to Pittsburgh."

Her Rutgers courses receive high student ratings, as do Frank's, but mass public speaking of the sort they must do on the Plains still unnerves her. On the upcoming trip, as on their previous excursions West, Deborah plans to run the overhead projector, do a statistical presentation, answer questions about it afterward, give Frank coaching notes on his performance, and pursue all-purpose diplomacy. She has learned to carry tissues in her purse on these speaking trips, to give to the farm women who come talk to her afterward and end up crying. Sometimes she cries too.

"I hate making people feel bad, I just *hate* it," she says. Her vowels are slow and sliding, nearly Southern, though she was born and raised on Manhattan's West Side.

That Plains audiences seem ready, even eager, to interpret the Buffalo Commons idea as a sinister confirmation of their area's decline—or as an out-by-Tuesday order to evacuate a beloved landscape—baffles and troubles both Poppers. They see the Commons as an affirmation, a second chance at doing right by a biosphere in distress.

"The counties that might form the initial core of a Buffalo Commons are depopulating briskly, with no help from us," Frank Popper insists. "We foresee no Mad Max, total-desolation scenario, but rather a continuing gradual pullback over several generations by the private sector—in other words, people exercising the right to vote with their feet—and then nature taking its course across an area the size of Montana."

The hired-gun nature of the planning consultant's life, along with five years spent running a large and sometimes fractious academic department, has accustomed Frank to turn-downs and foul-uppery; he is used to being hated. Deborah, after years as a reference librarian and doctoral candidate, is not. She tries not to flinch, much, from what her computer data packages have wrought. Without her county-by-county mappings of the Plains, a Buffalo Commons would remain speculative fiction. With them, it is scholarly and political nitroglycerin.

Many who turn out to hear them on the Plains assume that the Poppers are being paid to conduct such research. Actually, the Buffalo Commons is more an intellectual hobby that has gotten out of hand. The pair hold no grants for their work, no extra Rutgers funding, and no foundation or government support. When invited to a conference or forum they get plane fare and a few hundred dollars in speaking fees. "We prefer to remain unbought," says Frank politely.

Low-budget research is no novelty. The Popper clan spent the dry summer of 1985 driving thirty thousand miles of dusty back roads from Kansas to Montana in a dented 1978 Toyota (no air-conditioning) laden with economy-size jars of peanut butter. The parents walked fields, asked questions, took pictures, made notes. The children fought nightly over whose turn it was to occupy the motel bed closest to New Jersey. Throughout, Frank kept on the dashboard a copy of Walter Prescott Webb's 1931 study *The Great Plains*. Now he pulls the sun-battered paperback from his office bookshelf and passes it to me. Brown grit sifts from between the pages onto my hand.

In the scholarly universe, ideas, once released, are always alive. The Great Plains, intensively examined for over a century, are the subject of an immense literature. Today there are Plains institutes, Plains seminars, Plains conferences, Plains colloquia, journals of the Plains, museums of the Plains. Their harvest is always the same—ceaseless argument and no consensus. But ideas rule the American West, and always have. The

Poppers are engaged in an extended, across-the-generations conversation about the nature and function of this unruly region with four of its principal previous interpreters: Gilpin, Powell, and Turner, all working in the nineteenth century, and Webb, writing in the early twentieth.

William Gilpin is the patron saint of Western boosterism. A friend of Andrew Jackson who went exploring to the Pacific with Fremont in 1843, fought Mexicans and Pawnees, and spent time in Washington as an adviser on Western affairs to Senator Thomas Hart Benton of Missouri, Gilpin became, in the 1860s, Colorado's first territorial governor. He was also the best salesman the Plains ever had, a tireless promoter of the catch-phrase "Manifest Destiny." In speech after speech, book after book, he wove fantasies of frontier possibility, and seems to have believed every word.

A hundred million people eventually settling in the Missis-sippi Valley and points west? But of course, Gilpin claimed. He described the lands beyond the Missouri as magnificently fer-tile, the water table crying out for artesian wells, the tender prairie shrubs possessed of root systems so vast that settlers need only dig to find firewood. For each buffalo exterminated, three cows or sheep could be profitably pastured, on grassland so lush that seeds dropped onto the earth grew to effortless harvest. Sleeping outdoors was a year-round delight, given the Plains' temperate seasons, and the mountain-fed streams that coursed this Canaan were full of trout and gold. Surely the region was destined to nourish one of the world's great civilizations, like Babylon or Rome. Sign here.

In 1869 and in 1871–72, a young ethnographer and geologist named John Wesley Powell was commissioned by Congress to examine the rapidly opening West and its agricultural prospects.

Powell believed in progress as much as the next Victorian, and more than some, but his report on the arid lands is a Federalist Papers of American land use, its message direct and fervent: *Please* don't do this.

Or if we must settle the prairies and desert and intermountain region, Powell argued, let us be adaptive. Resurvey the West, not in neat grids but according to the lay of the land, so that everyone gets a bit of water frontage and decent soil. Try water-rights cooperatives; it worked for the Mormons. Try common cattle-grazing areas, as the Spanish had been doing in New Mexico since the seventeenth century on land just as dry. Make the minimum grant for an unirrigated farm 2,560 acres, four square miles, not the quarter-section that Jefferson felt suitable for the American yeoman. Jefferson's agricultural model works best where the land is abundant in trees, topsoil, and rainfall. East of the Mississippi, 160 acres made a productive pioneer homestead. But, said Powell, you break your back and your heart applying Eastern rules to buffalo country.

Powell's *Report on the Lands of the Arid Region of the United States* is ancestor to much conservation and land-use thought, but in the late 1870s it never made it out of committee. The House eventually approved a pallid version, and even that was disputed to the last by Western politicians and speculators and corporations and land and cattle and water barons, whose push for development and Gilpinesque PR were so flatly contradicted by Powell's footsore realism.

Further skewing the land-use fate of the Plains was unusually fine weather during the initial settlement years. For nearly two thrilling decades, wheatfields really did rise golden, small towns flourished, immigrants poured in, and Powell looked like an alarmist, a willful obstructor of Manifest Destiny. If the prairie was not yet a garden, its cultivation at least seemed a workable proposition, a triumph of human will over the wishes of the land. But early in the 1880s the droughts began, and locust swarms, too. The word "blizzard" was coined to describe the unprecedented winter storms on the Plains in the 1870s and 1880s. Dryland farming techniques for wheat, widely introduced in the nineties, came too late for many. Plains towns and farms started emptying out by 1890. To this ongoing tale of Plains depopulation, the Buffalo Commons is the far-end conjecture.

Eighteen-ninety stands as a cenotaph in any Great Plains time line. It was a year of endings, readjustments, redefinitions. Fully loaded wagon trains could be sighted going east all that year, carrying defeated homesteaders back across the 98th meridian. At the Standing Rock agency on South Dakota's Pine Ridge Reservation, Sioux shamans and tribespeople circled and chanted, believing that the Ghost Dance, done well and faithfully, would aid the return of their ancestral dead, sweeping away the white world and returning the buffalo to the Plains. On the other hand, in Washington, D.C., the Census Bureau announced that if the frontier were defined as area with a population density of less than two people per square mile, then as of 1890 the frontier was no more.

Learning this, the University of Wisconsin (later Harvard) historian Frederick Jackson Turner began writing a paper (delivered at the Columbian Exposition in Chicago in 1893) about the effect of the frontier on America's vision of itself. As successive waves of settlers reached and moved beyond the line of known territory, Turner said, the act of claiming a continent encouraged in the national personality a restless, practical, exuberant, violence-prone individualism. Without frontier, he worried, we would be a less interesting, less effective nation.

Turner's definition of frontier employed the two-person-per-square-mile rule invoked by the Census Bureau. Ninety-four years later Frank Popper noted in the *Yale Review* that as of 1980, 143 Western counties again fitted that definition. The population of such counties is very small, one American out of every 396, a population density so light that the Eastern equivalent would be a Manhattan Island inhabited by at most 46 souls. But frontier counties still total an area of 949,500 square miles, or over a quarter of the United States. "We are no longer a frontier nation, but we are still a nation with a frontier," Frank says, addressing Turner's ghost. "We will become more of one as the Buffalo Commons emerges."

Walter Prescott Webb, a historian at the University of Texas, is the fourth voice in this long-range conversation. Webb produced his masterwork, *The Great Plains*, just before the 1930s Dust Bowl. Webb chronicled the ways in which settlers sought to adapt to a new region that was level, arid, and treeless. Elsewhere, culture "stood on three legs—land, water and timber." In the Plains, "not one but two of these legs were withdrawn—water and timber—and civilization was left on one leg—land. It is small wonder that it toppled over in temporary failure." Webb was speaking mainly of the crises of the 1880s and 1890s, but similar failure cycles, which seem to confirm this pattern of boom and bust, have occurred in the 1930s and in the 1980s and 1990s.

The question of just how temporary such failures are still leads to violent quarrels in and out of academe. And Webb's other famous image, of Plains settlements as "islands in a shortgrass sea," disturbs as many as it reassures. Those who live on the

Plains, and those who study them, frequently invoke the "half a glass of water" simile to describe conditions there. The heirs of Gilpin insist the glass is at least half full, the islands sturdily self-sufficient.

I gather a stack of the Poppers' Commons correspondence and take it to a Rutgers conference room to read. I sift through letters from farmers in Saskatchewan and Manitoba, attesting to parallel Canadian depopulations and declines in sections of the prairie provinces. Other letters are from old people on the Plains, many written in tremulous but still-lovely Spencerian penmanship, recalling diphtheria and grassfires and lard sandwiches when the crops failed. Two friendly notes from North Dakota, one assuring the Poppers that three out of four extraterrestrials agree the Plains are doomed. Lots of buffalo-care queries. The Poppers have learned more than they ever wanted about the habits of the ungulate, or hoofed mammal, *Bison bison*, also known as *Bison americanus*. One letter, from New London, Connecticut, I take back and read to Frank:

Dear Professors Popper,
Since you are well-known experts on these matters, what do you recommend as a good warm bran mash for yearling buffalo? What do you feed yours?

"Where does he think we keep them, in the basement?" mutters Frank.

When I return yet another armload of Commons correspondence to his office later that afternoon, Frank is on the phone, leaning perilously far back in his aged swivel chair and looking out the window. He is talking with Cloyd Clark, the Nebraska judge who will host part of their upcoming visit to the Plains. Frank and Deborah are scheduled for a public lecture and forum in McCook, Nebraska, near the Kansas border. Then a research expedition into backcountry Nebraska and Colorado. Then on to Denver, to debate the Buffalo Commons concept at the annual national convention of American planners. They are flying to Nebraska; two days earlier, I will catch a plane to Omaha, then ride the night train across the state and meet them in McCook.

"Sure, sure, sure," Frank Popper says into the receiver. He is a rat-tat-tat talker, gulping breaths between ideas, waving his arms to indicate the cresting of a notion.

"We'll answer questions, whatever you like, right, fine, stay as long as people can stand us."

He thumps upright but keeps on listening, hands busy with papers and offprints and yellow pads. Graduate students wander past the open door, gossiping about deadlines. A computer printer chatters in the next room. In mid-sort, Frank Popper's hands stop.

"*How* many security people did you say?" He listens again. "Yes. Well. That sounds extreme. I know people are upset, but don't you think—"

The Nebraska judge's reply makes Frank sigh. Suddenly he looks much older than his forty-six years. "All right, half a dozen sheriff's deputies. Whatever. Just don't tell Deborah."

But Deborah is already standing in the doorway of the chairman's office, hugging a sheaf of photocopies to her burgundy jumper with one hand and with the other pushing back her pepper-and-salt bangs in a gesture of incredulity and dismay.

I look from one to the other, several times, but they still

resemble a mild and conscientious academic couple, sub-scribers to the *New York Review of Books*, alumni of Harvard and Bryn Mawr, familiars of card catalogues, chauffeurs of junior-high sports teams. They do not seem the sort of people whose research presentations require armed bodyguards.

II
THE GHOST
DANCERS

THE CENTRAL PLAINS:
Nebraska,
Kansas,
Colorado

"**M**cCOOK!" SAID MY UNCLE EDWARD, shaking his head. He stared out the door of the Omaha train station into the black air of a cold May night. "McCook," he repeated, punching each syllable with the precision of distaste, and worry. Plains English is an inflected tongue, like Mandarin, and I could hear the subtext clearly: *So, have you made out your will?* Like many residents of the eastern sections of Great Plains states, my uncle clearly considered the lands past the 98th meridian a suspect terrain. Nothing out there till you hit the Rocky Mountains; five hundred miles of nothing. Maybe some cows. Maybe a jackrabbit.

"McCook's way the hell on the other side of the state," he informed me. "I've *been* to McCook. There's zero there. You're sure you want to do this?"

The 12:40 A.M. Amtrak to Denver, a double-decker, had just arrived with a flourish of bells and air brakes, and conductors were urging passengers into the cars. A Native American teenager in Navy uniform brushed by me, followed by four firm-stepping old men in Stetsons. Then a farm family, staggering under bags of stonewashed jeans and CDs and coffee makers and Godiva chocolate, loot from the malls of Omaha. It all looked fairly sedate, but as the train pulled out, Ed was still frowning.

It takes five long hours to cross Nebraska by train, following the Burlington and Missouri River track laid in the 1870s across the state's southern third. Packed like an emigrant boxcar, the Amtrak *Zephyr* sways along, leaving behind Omaha's freeways and office towers, curving south to the university city of Lincoln, then hurrying west, and west some more, an orange moon sinking lower and lower as we go. At three in the morning the train halts in Hastings. Under a light pole a solitary pickup waits. At Holdrege, sixty miles later, we stop again. No one boards, and no one gets off.

From the train window I can see only blackness, but I know our route is cutting across Nebraska's growing zones. Near Omaha the brown topsoil, or mollisol, of glacial till and wind-deposited silt is nearly a hundred feet deep. This gift of the last ice age spreads well past the middle of the state; I have stood in cornfields near Grand Island in July and heard the stalks growing in this rich dark loess, a juicy whisper in the humid air. But McCook (pop. 8,000) lies well into the dry Plains, where the soil is often paler, younger, and lower-nutrient—but still good wheat country, and good rangeland for sheep- and cattle-grazing.

In the dark, swaying train, my head jerks out of sleep, falls back, jerks again. At five-thirty in the morning, as the Amtrak cars pull away from McCook for Fort Morgan, Colorado, I am grateful that the Chief Motel offers limo service. Susie the night maid is waiting with her station wagon, and we roar up McCook's main drag as the stars dissolve overhead into a flawless dawn sky.

McCook epitomizes the self-contained service center favored by Deborah Popper's computers for long-term survival. Even if the population around it continues to thin, McCook will likely remain a hub for southwestern Nebraska, the northwest corner of Kansas, and the northwest edge of Colorado. I have just seen one reason, the daily Amtrak. McCook also lobbied for, and got, United Airlines and GP Air feeder service. It has a golf course, a CAT scanner, a community college, and a splendid early Frank Lloyd Wright house. From the lumberyards, farm-supply dealers, and cowboy bars that line the flats beside the Republican River, McCook's business district stretches up a half-mile hillside to the residential areas at blufftop, where shady streets are lined with frame houses—all neat, a few grand—set back on wide lots. A five-bedroom Victorian in the best neighborhood sells for $45,000 and up.

I talk to Henry Booher, a retired smokestack-industry executive, originally from Missouri, who runs the one-man McCook Industrial Development Corporation. He and his wife considered the Ozarks, Santa Fe, and Idaho for retirement but chose McCook, "for aesthetic reasons. We like the prairie. If you were raised as I was, in a small town, the appeal of a community like this is strong, even—maybe especially—after a life in the corporate world. Yes, many in western Nebraska feel the slippery slope of decline, the inability to compete, but not much gets these people excited, except golf. The farmers are golf-mad. They drive fifty or seventy-five miles here to play."

He has been trying to attract light industry to Red Willow County ("Every little town between Utah and Massachusetts is giving away the farm to attract an electronics or printing plant," he says, sighing). McCook plans to bid for a new four-hundred-inmate state prison, which would mean about 140 local jobs. He would also like to expand local tourism, that being Nebraska's second-largest industry. McCook in hunting season is a madhouse, he assures me, with hunters arriving hourly from

Denver and Texas to stalk mule deer, cottontail rabbits, wild turkey, ringneck pheasant, and quail.

I tour the beautifully equipped forty-four-bed hospital, whose ten doctors do mostly family practice, and a lot of it, plus the occasional tractor accident. Four of the nine surrounding counties have no M.D.'s at all. If a specialist is needed, they fly one in from Lincoln or Omaha. "The organ-retrieval service loves to get Nebraska organs for transplants," Janet Fidler, a registered nurse from McCook, tells me proudly. "Ours is very healthy land. No AIDS, no bad air, no crowding. And no crime." (The McCook police blotter bears her out; offenses for the previous week include three intoxicated underage males, all released to parents; several speeding tickets; and one woman hauled in for littering.)

Supermarket lines here are full of cowboys, some with the big gold tooled belt buckles of rodeo champions. They wait patiently with shopping baskets of Evian and oat-bran doughnuts, and drive away in dusty Hondas. The larger world seems less alien to many in west Nebraska than does their own nation's East Coast. "How long do you get to stay in the United States before you have to go back to New York?" is a favorite pleasantry.

Henry Booher, the development head, has just helped one McCook veterinary-supply firm expand its markets into Australia and New Zealand. In the last year the president of the local irrigation district has traveled to Russia and the Mediterranean. Farm owners expound on European trade barriers after 1992, and on our falling share in the world grain market as Canada, Australia, and Argentina all increase production. The president of McCook's trim two-year college dreams of importing Japanese students. Does he also dream of managing some more imposing campus? Standing by his four-wheel drive he squints in the strong prairie sun. "I like small," he says simply.

Still, the McCook population is not much higher now than in 1960, and over a hundred residents are being bused 156 miles a day roundtrip to work at the new meatpacking plant in Lexington, two counties away, and grateful for it. Lift up your eyes incautiously in McCook, and past the immaculate brick streets an immensity of bare buttes rises at the edge of town. Everyone speaks freely of the need for self-reliance in a difficult land, less quickly of the loneliness that can settle on the spirit here. At lunch with the college staffers and Judge Cloyd Clark (a big-boned McCookian who favors bolo ties, rousing arguments, and stringent sentencing), I pick up some excellent tips on surviving a car breakdown in Nebraska's desolate backcountry when night is coming and the windchill is seventy below.

"Anyone who tries to cross the Nebraska Sand Hills in winter without long underwear, a blanket, a shovel, and an emergency kit is a *fool*," says Clark, which is correct. In the restaurant parking lot I meet the wife of another community college administrator, hauling podium decorations from her car trunk for the Poppers' talk. She retains the buffalo skull but allows me to carry the buffalo robe, forty unwieldy pounds of hide and lustrous brown pelt. She is an ex–New Yorker who used to live in Greenwich Village. "Sometimes I ride and ride my racing bike west toward Boulder, Colorado," she tells me, "and pretend I can get there, if I just pedal hard enough."

Jeffrey Aaronson, the photographer assigned to do the pictures for the newspaper story I am preparing on the Poppers, arrives in the early afternoon from Aspen, his home base. His fashionable curls, electric-blue and black shirt buttoned to the neck, and monstrous satchel of Nikons mesmerize downtown McCook.

Jeffrey is thirty-four, hyperactive, hyperarticulate, hyperalert. He tells me he gave up doctoral work in biochemistry for the photojournalist's life.

We drive west, scouting locations, looking, he tells me, for good light. Everything we pass—windmills against the sky, grain elevators, sheds with peeling paint—he assesses for picture potential. He is also considering a helicopter or small-plane charter, to get some aerial shots of prairie. A very abandoned gas station with a green and gold DeKalb corn sign askew on its roof inspires a U-turn.

"Look at the symbolism! What a folk artifact: the winged ear of corn, the downward orientation!" It takes some time to persuade him that seed-corn ads are as mundane in Nebraska as trash on the streets in New York. As the country beyond McCook flattens out and begins to look more (but not enough) like the broad, featureless terrain that Manhattan photo editors crave, he tells of living by his wits in mainland China, of photographing remote temples for *National Geographic*, of fighting through the crowds in Tiananmen Square for closeups of student protestors. We swerve to the gravel shoulder to inspect a handmade placard there, stout black characters on peeling white board: "We trust," it reads, "that land and money will never again be wasted in Nebraska, as it was on this stretch of road. Tecker Ranch."

A side road runs up a rise on the highway's south side. On impulse we turn off and mount the hill, and half the Central Plains lie magnificently before us, not flat at all but a complicated weave of terraced fields, thrush-gray and olive and bright green and rust, with bright towers of cumulus riding overhead. The late-afternoon sun defines every erosion gully; and there are hundreds, in stark purple shadow.

THE GHOST DANCERS

A John Deere tractor with a glassed-in cab appears around the curve of the closest hill, tilting as it follows the flow of the land, and we bound toward it through waist-high weeds, shouting and waving. The driver is Kenny McDonald, a hired man for Jerry and Cindy Fries. The Fries farm keeps 800 acres in dryland wheat, 1,000 in irrigated alfalfa. At forty-five, small and tough, McDonald looks sixty. This is Kansas you're in, he tells us kindly; Cheyenne County, Kansas. He has always lived here and says he might well drive over to McCook tonight to see the Poppers out of curiosity, though a lot of people are asking, why pay $4 admission to hear we're all going to be taken off the land by the federal government?

"Hard work is *everything*," he tells us, after a pause for thought, sitting on the cultivator bar of his tractor. "And, of course, rain." Work-battered hands marked with blisters, cuts, and blackened nails press down on overalled knees. "Give up this land? No, no, no, no, no. Those New Jersey professors will have a fight on their hands."

Could he pause at the far end of the field on his next pass around and wait for Jeffrey's signal, so the tractor will give the pictures scale? McDonald is willing. He takes it all very calmly, these odd pleas from anxious, sweaty strangers. The huge piece of farm machinery trundles off, leaving us awash in the scent of turned earth and uprooted grasses. An enormous cloud bank obscures the sun, and Jeffrey paces, cursing, adjusting lenses and exposures, knowing that Kenny McDonald's good nature or the west wind or both may give out and make him lose the shot.

Then his pacing slows, and eventually he stands still, looking for a long time at the hundred-mile view. He sits down near me on the hillside, cradling the camera, eyes flicking from the waiting land to the problem of the cloud and back again. Our city shoes are mired with Cheyenne County mud, our sleeves are a collage of last year's burrs. For long minutes, among the bindweed and buffalo grass, we wait, watching the great cloud sail slowly over the sun, seeing the colors of the fields sharpen and dim and sharpen again in the living light.

"My grandfather was a peddler in South Dakota," Jeffrey says suddenly. "He knew this land. Then he made it out to L.A. and never saw it again. I wonder if he was ever sorry?"

Deborah Popper looks distinctly sorry that evening as she and Frank climb stiffly out of a very small aircraft. She has been on too many aging planes in uncertain weather since they acquired this pastime. Frank is in bounding spirits, thrilled to be out of New Jersey. "This is really very exotic," he says, surveying the grassland beside the airstrip and inhaling pure, dry prairie air. Outside their room at the Chief Motel a modeling school is in session, rock music thumping as a dozen teenage Nebraskans walk a makeshift runway beside the indoor pool. The boys are in dinner jackets, the girls in off-the-shoulder formals. All look extremely husky, nervous, polite, and blond.

The Poppers' presentation packs the McCook High School auditorium with nearly four hundred people, an impressive turnout for a warm Saturday night at the end of calving season. Attendees from four states (Colorado, Kansas, Nebraska, and South Dakota) fill the velveteen tip-up chairs. There are lots of ties in evidence, lots of pearl necklaces. A bouquet of prairie grasses and the buffalo robe adorn the stage. Judge Cloyd Clark stalks the aisles, looking delighted. He is the only one who does.

Frank Popper's talk is received with absolute and unsmiling attention. Expecting a wild man, the crowd gets instead a sober Harvard Ph.D. in a dark gray pinstripe suit, delivering a calm, formal accounting of land-use patterns with special attention to where myth and statistics collide.

He tells them their own story, the tale of the forgotten semi-arid fifth of the continental United States. No one state, he reminds them, lies completely within the Plains; consider the difficulties—cultural, political, educational, economic—created by having, in effect, two Nebraskas, lying east and west of the anhydrous line. The entire population of the Plains is about that of Georgia. The largest city actually on the Plains is Lubbock, Texas (pop. 173,000), and the second-largest is Billings, Montana (pop. 67,000).

It is an unusual region, he continues, with a history of excess and scarcity. Boom leads to overplanting and overgrazing, which lead to bust, which leads to depopulation. Already the Plains have been through three such cycles, and they are starting on a fourth. The first cycle ran from the Homestead Act of 1862 through the cattle drives of the 1880s and the financial panic and drought of the 1890s. The early 1900s brought new homesteading laws, but from 1920 on a recurrence of drought and locusts put the Plains into depression well before 1929. The 1930s saw the catastrophe of the Dust Bowl, and Okies as a vivid symbol of Plains depopulation.

In the mid-twentieth century, Frank continues, conditions were briefly better. The Plains were poor but economically viable, due mostly to a heavy injection of federal subsidies. Through the 1970s there was energetic sodbusting, ten thousand acres at a time. Gas and oil boomtowns dotted the Northern Plains. But the eighties punctured it all, revealing the fragility of extractive (and quite possibly finite) economies. Now ghost towns are forming everywhere on the Plains, as the little settlements that once sustained the region lose doctor, bus stop, bank, stores, air service, clergy, young people.

But this time around, Frank argues, almost pleading with them now, this time the cycle of decline is different, and worse.

Other contributing factors have appeared: the greenhouse effect, shifts in foreign policy that mean missile-base closings across the Plains, shifts in world agriculture markets, even the change in American diets, away from red meat. Certainly the Plains have a historic mission as the granary of last resort, for the United States and for the world. But the real problem is slow-leak depopulation. Some places will get by on the twenty-first-century Plains: service centers like McCook; those in the shadow of urban areas, or near interstates, or where traditional mining or agriculture economies stay viable. But many others will not make it.

Deborah, at the overhead projector, slides onto the auditorium screen a map of Plains counties in significant land-use distress, the same map I saw in the computer lab at Rutgers. There are audible gasps, then a rising hum of defiance and dread. Many heads in the audience suddenly bow or are proudly raised. Couples feel for each other's hands. At the next display— Nebraska counties in land-use distress—there are audible murmurs of "Oh, my God," as people half rise out of their seats in the semidarkness to spot their home areas.

"Like waiting for SAT scores," whispers a high school boy in the row behind me.

"I ain't selling," calls a rancher, from the rear of the room. Another rancher bounces on booted toes, too agitated to sit.

"Holy cow," he says, "holy cow." For a Nebraska Lutheran, this is very strong language. "These folks really hate us. This is grim. We're really getting beat on."

Frank is talking again. So what shall we do? One solution is a Buffalo Commons. The 110 distressed counties just shown would be the nucleus. Much of the land in such areas is no longer even under cultivation. And many other potential building blocks are already in place—thousands of properties foreclosed by the Farmers Home Administration and the Farm Credit System and private banks; lands in the Department of Agriculture's Conservation Reserve program, which pays farmers not to cultivate marginal land; holdings of the Interior Department's Bureau of Land Management; acreage held in trust by environmental groups such as the Nature Conservancy; state parks and preserves; and the nineteen national grasslands already managed by the Forest Service. A Buffalo Commons could even coexist with population growth in the Plains cities and service centers. It could be expanded beyond the counties in land-use distress that the Poppers' maps identify.

On most of the Plains, life would go on as it always has. But in other parts of the region, the buffalo would indeed roam—and Japanese and German and French and U.S. tour buses, too.

The Poppers sit down in the auditorium's front row as local panelists rise to reply: Sue Renken, a banker from Enders; Ervain Friehe, a wheat grower from near McCook; Jack Maddux, a Wauneta rancher and candidate for lieutenant governor; Jane Renner Hood, the executive director of the Nebraska Humanities Council. Each rebuttal is punctuated with angry cheers. Everywhere they speak the Poppers encounter a pattern of outrage that they have come to call the Four Responses: Pioneer Gumption (Don't underestimate determination and hard work), Dollar Potential (Plains food production can still feed the world), Eastern Ignorance (self-explanatory), and Prairie Zen (Our landscape is a powerful source of spiritual renewal).

All are in operation now. The banker, peppy and blonde, describes her afternoon rides with the family cattle herds. After hardworking hours in the saddle, she says, she always feels overwhelmingly peaceful and happy. Shouts of agreement drown her next sentences. Over the tumult, she cries, "I love our Plains!" The political candidate makes New Jersey jokes and reminds the audience of Nebraska's innovative legislation, the most restrictive in the nation, to keep family farms from takeover by agribusiness land cartels. The historian passionately quotes the nineteenth-century Sioux mystic Black Elk on the enduring glory of the Great Plains—"the beautiful land of our fathers, forever green and clear." As she finishes, the crowd explodes with righteous hurrahs and applause.

The Poppers exchange glances.

"Everyone loves to cite Black Elk out here," Frank whispers to me. "I can't imagine why. His memoirs are probably in large part a work of semifiction by a white anthropologist. Why cling so to a text that foretells the vanishing of the white way and the return of the buffalo? It's completely nonadaptive. These farmers and ranchers don't want to know it yet, but in the contemporary West *they* are the new Indians. We seem to be cast as the new Crazy Horse, speaking in visions. Or as the twentieth-century intellectual version of the Ghost Dance. What a mind-warp!" He heaves himself up to take questions from the house.

A farmer wants to know why the Commons proposal ignores the states. An insurance agent from North Platte accuses the Poppers of betraying the principle of the land-grant university by emphasizing depressing data rather than researching ways to improve life on the Plains.

Frank tries to explain that academic planners think a great deal about states—states as self-regulating entities, personifying the home-rule concept of "Every tub on its own bottom"; and also states as the beneficiaries of research done at their perennially undersupported land-grant colleges, the boundaries of the public university in most cases truly being the boundaries of the state. But what real good is a land-grant school in the long run, he continues, if uncomfortable discoveries are hidden from the very taxpayers who pay professorial salaries?

"Nice answers, stop there," Deborah mutters beside me, but her husband is just warming up. In fact, he says, starting to stride back and forth behind the lectern, states are quite artificial constructs, and not always useful ones. Colorado—half prairie, half mountains—is a *terrible* idea. All the Plains states are terrible ideas, ecologically speaking. This line of argument does not go over well.

As the evening's moderator, the marketing manager of the Decatur County Feed Yard (Oberlin, Kansas), begins to wrap up, Frank mutters, "I feel I'm failing as a communicator."

Deborah nods.

Not everyone in the room shares this pessimism. "They do pretty effective teaching," comments Charlie Gregory, an instructor at McCook Community College, as he watches the crowd hand in comment sheets at the close of the presentation and walk out stony-faced, like people leaving a battleground, or a wake. "This part of the country responds to unemotional fact, not Donahue, and that's what they got. Before tonight, about seventy-five percent were dead set against the Poppers. Now it's probably thirty-five percent."

The completed questionnaires suggest some private doubts behind the public rhetoric of denial. From a resident of Hermosa, South Dakota (pop. 251):

"Terrifyingly logical."

Three responses from McCook:

"Stupid."

"Good facts, wrong conclusions."

"Better pray for rain—or all move to New Jersey."

Four from western Kansas:

"Maybe a hundred years ago this would make sense, now, no."

"I think we should be listening, very carefully, and live within our limits."

"I believe they documented their thesis."

"We all see the decline, but refuse to acknowledge it."

From Danbury, Nebraska (pop. 143):

"I suspect they're right, if only by accident."

Others in the audience are less easy to convince.

"There are only three things worth fighting for—life, liberty, and land!" cries Paul D. Ornan, a forty-five-year-old farmer from Maywood, Nebraska. Ornan climbs over a row of seats, vaults the steps between auditorium and podium, and advances on a sweating Frank Popper, backing him step by step across the wooden stage. Frank is five foot ten, but Ornan's flushed face looms four furious inches above his. Half a dozen uniformed sheriff's deputies, hands on holsters, move toward professor and challenger. Ornan is shouting, and many in the departing crowd turn to stare, some shocked, some grinning.

"Don't try to come in and use our land for common property for people from New Jersey and California. *Don't you do that!*"

Frank opens his mouth, then closes it again; Ornan is trembling with anger and far from done. "If they want my land," he announces, enunciating with extreme care, hands convulsively opening and shutting, "they'll have to shoot me and drag me away!"

"Hmm, well, interesting point," says Frank in his best department chair's voice, trying to calm the farmer, but Ornan will not be soothed; he is ushered into the Nebraska twilight still muttering about East Coast conspiracies. "When you're threatened, you have to respond," he explains to his escort, loudly, on the way up the aisle to the exit.

"Dear, I thought you were dead meat there," says Deborah, trying to maintain her poise, trying to smile and not succeeding.

Frank Skinner, an officer with the McCook sheriff's department, apologizes, and so do a half-dozen other people standing by. A few minutes later Skinner stands on the high school lawn, watching Frank and Deborah (both still a little subdued) walking toward Cloyd Clark's car under the cottonwoods that shadow the tidy residential street, each house with a porch light, each porch with a welcome mat.

"The Poppers are right," he says softly. In the warm twilight his thin, kind face is sad and knowing. "With closed minds we'll get nowhere. A lot of the land is going, and it just breaks your heart."

Wherever the Poppers speak on the Plains the region's Darwinian history springs to disturbing life. In a Rutgers seminar room the Buffalo Commons can remain a controlled intellectual exercise. But the postmodern Plains strongly suspect they are perceived by the rest of America as a lesser land—interchangeable rectangular dung-colored states—and resentments build, and build. With some reason: when a 1990 Rand McNally travel atlas, for reasons of space, omitted North Dakota, South Dakota, and Oklahoma, the editor explained blithely that Plains states seemed least likely to be missed.

In these wars of place, Plains animosity is directed almost wholly northeastward. The Eastern Seaboard is ritually scorned on the Plains, at all social and income levels, as a land of yammerers who have never seen a prime-time pig-feed commercial, or heard a tornado warning siren. California, by contrast, has long carried a covert fascination, because hundreds of thousands of Plains residents desperate for agricultural or defense jobs fled there in the 1930s and 1940s. Very few returned. (For years in Pierre, rumors persisted about a wondrous Los Angeles event called South Dakota Day, a Valhallan reunion by the Pacific where state expatriates turned up in splendid cars and congratulated one another on getting the hell out of Murdo.)

Faulkner's observation that the past isn't dead, it isn't even past, is confirmed by every crowd the Poppers address. Great Plains people, exalted and trapped by their curious history, are belligerently loyal to ancestral suffering; resentful of, yet dependent on, outside assistance; profoundly suspicious of fancy language, change, and choice. "Down-to-earth" and "practical" are compliments. Actions are what count as revealers of truth. "Talks too much" is profound condemnation, about the worst you can say of anyone. The next-worst adjective for a person or an idea is "different," as in "That's real . . . different."

For a hundred years the Plains, through brutal necessity, have recognized only two sorts of people: those who leave, and those who stay. Though I grew up in Wisconsin and now live in New Jersey, I am marginally respectable in McCook because my great-great-grandfather Andersson sat out the Long Winter of 1881 in a South Dakota claim shanty; because my grandmother McDonnell was born to a pioneer family near Hartington, Nebraska, in 1900, and never saw an ocean till she was seventy. The Poppers are . . . real different.

Worse, they talk for a living; talk for pleasure; talk to help. One of the principal cultural barriers in Frank and Deborah's self-imposed mission to educate a region is the Ivy League/research university policy-analysis style itself, whose cool and rigorous language traditionally permits no excuses, leaves nowhere to hide. Its impersonal realism in laying out options and predicting outcomes can sound, to the uninitiated ear, like cruelty. Institute A, mandate B, and interesting results will occur; observe the decisive variables, suggest a course of action, ah, yes, a whole region down the drain, remarkable scholarship, next case.

Nothing in their professional or personal histories warned the Poppers of the Plains' unreasoning terror of talk, and change, and talking about change. "In vain" is the hardest Popper message of all. At the buffet supper after the McCook talk, a Colorado feedlot owner corners Frank.

"Asking us to admit that we were wrong all along, in trying to settle a lot of this country, is like asking us to have surgery without anesthetic." Better preventive medicine now, Frank retorts, than wholesale disaster later. They stare at each other over the three-pepper coleslaw and kiwi salad, in mutual incomprehension and despair.

The next morning, very early, the Poppers and the photographer Jeffrey Aaronson and I drive northwest from McCook, heading for the adjoining county of Hayes. Two-thirds the size of Rhode Island, Hayes County has a population of 1,200 and is very high on the Poppers' endangered list. This is the deep Plains, a minimalist landscape of sun, wind, and grass. We drive for an hour and see eight houses, no billboards, and no human beings. All of us know that by August these greening fields and flowering roadsides will be bleached and baked to yellow dryness, but soft days like this almost make Great Plains winters worth enduring.

"Frank, remember getting stuck in that blizzard last year for six hours, trying to get to your talk in Aberdeen?" asks Deborah, watching a ring-necked pheasant whir up from the tall roadside grasses. "And remember the huge ice storms when we were doing research in Rolette County, North Dakota? I *knew* we might need those thermal gloves, and I was right." For a moment, she sounds almost like Cloyd Clark.

We pull over. Jeffrey, determined to catch the splendid raking light, urges the Poppers through a barbed-wire fence and toward an enormous rolled haybale in the distance. Left behind to guard the van—from what, it is hard to say, since we have not seen a soul in miles—I look around, and around, and around, turning full circle in search of topography, but I discover only a horizon line. Decidedly, we have located flat Nebraska.

Atop the haybale, two plowed fields away, Frank and Deborah are tiny figures with attaché cases, standing, turning, sitting at the photographer's gestured command. There is almost too much light, distance, and air in this morning world of limited palette—dun, gray-green, pale gold—and limitless skies. Except for fenceposts and phone poles, there is no built object here, and no made sound. The silence beats and rings on my eardrums.

Deborah climbs back through the barbed-wire fence, looking balefully at her high heels, followed by Frank, who is reciting Kerouac: "Oh, the wild, lyrical, drizzling air of Nebraska!" We all look at him warily, then return to the drive, and the view. Before this clear, warm morning, Hayes County was only a set of data entries on a Rutgers computer screen to the Poppers. Frank peers around with interest at the land he has publicly declared prime Buffalo Commons territory. A few miles later I ask him what he sees.

"A severe landscape, made humanly more severe," he replies, pointing to serpentine gullies forty feet deep. "A dispassionate place. The ecological system is extremely degraded. In

1870 we'd count six dozen varieties of grasses here, instead of the current two or three. And lots more game. This country is perfectly suited to buffalo, not a monoculture of wheat or corn."

The prairies—tallgrass, midgrass, and shortgrass—are the most disrupted ecosystem in North America. Before 1850 prairie defined the heart of the continent, from southern Wisconsin to western Montana, from central Texas to the Dakotas. In wet periods the spectacular tallgrass of the prairie's eastern edge might advance deeper into midgrass territory (where the growth averaged two to four feet rather than four and more); in bad years the hardier shortgrasses, which roll to the foot of the Rockies, might expand their range. Less than 1 percent of original prairie survived the plow. Nearly all such land—about 289,000 acres—is now preserved in national parks or monuments on the Great Plains, such as the Theodore Roosevelt National Park near Medora, North Dakota, or Custer State Park in western South Dakota.

A prairie excels at survival. The narrow, upright leaves of many prairie plants prevent overheating in these shadeless lands, as in-rolled leaves efficiently hold moisture. Prairie-grass seedlings spend their energy growing roots. A prairie is dense with information, two-thirds of it underground, invested in a massive root system that can reach six to ten feet below the topsoil. A square meter of shortgrass, composed chiefly of blue grama and buffalo grass, may contain five miles of roots, which is why the original sod was so hard to break. Pioneers said the prairie literally rang, or twanged, when the steel plows turned over its dense underlayer—"a storm of wild music," one wheat-farmer's child recalled, many decades later.

But the extreme stubbornness of grass roots is why a prairie is hard to transplant, and hard to subdue; why former grassland grows crops so well for the first few years, as the nutrients uncovered are used up in a burst of vegetative energy; why a prairie, left to itself, survives and even requires fire. Its plant tops are annual; their roots, perennial. Fire stimulates nitrogen release in the thin, dry soil, and a fire on the prairie, whether caused by lightning or controlled burns, only makes the next growth of native grasses richer.

Once its roots are broken, once its recovery cycle is interrupted by conventional agriculture, a grassland never heals unaided. The prairie ecosystem is so vulnerable to outside disturbance that the wheel ruts of the great western migration are still visible on its surface, more than 140 years after the covered wagons went west, heading to places like Hayes Center, Nebraska (pop. 231).

In Hayes Center, the seat of Hayes County, you can stand in the middle of town, look in any direction, and see prairie. Most of the one- and two-story buildings in its business district are boarded up and weather-battered, but on Saturday morning Hayes Center is as bustling as it gets. A half-dozen shoppers stroll in overalls and jogging suits. A lone Big Apple T-shirt is worn by a large twenty-seven-year-old named Mike Apple, who teaches history at the forty-four–student high school and lived last in San Jose, California.

"The four words people out here hate most are 'shutting up the land.' It strikes them as criminal," he says earnestly to the Poppers. "Listen, instead of importing buffalo, let's bring in old people instead, from the cities, to replace the kids that are leaving. Get that SSI income, see, into the Nebraska economy."

"Ummmnh," says Deborah—her repertoire of noncommittal noises has tripled in the last forty-eight hours—and she writes it down.

Hayes Center seems to be populated by citizens who have managed to fly under the radar of civilization and prefer it that way.

"I got tired of being mugged and came to western Nebraska by covered U-Haul," explains Johnny Scott, a wiry man in his middle forties. Formerly an office manager in Washington, D.C., and Jacksonville, Florida, he now owns Hayes Center's one grocery store, the hub of town activity. A sign in its window advertises a special on Nintendo rentals. Ocia Weston, seventy-six, on his way to the tiny post office, nods hard. He has lived here all his life. "The Poppers know nothing about us. No way will Hayes County go back to buffalo."

He agrees to have his picture taken. "For the McCook paper, is it?" No, says Jeffrey, apologetically, setting up his tripod, the *New York Times*. Mr. Weston, disappointed but polite, plants his stub-toed work shoes firmly on the cracking sidewalk, pulls his cap to a more rakish angle, and prepares to walk past a row of decrepit board structures for the photographer's benefit. "Cue me, son," he orders crisply. Jeffrey blinks, and obeys.

The local banker, wearing a green feed cap with a Miller Lite logo and carrying a copy of the *Wall Street Journal* under his arm, emerges from his office to stare across the street at the Poppers. Frank is examining a row of deserted buildings, as rapt as if touring Tibet, while Deborah snaps pictures of the town for use as slides in her American Geography course.

"I'm surprised they have the nerve to show up here," says Van Korell. He heard them talk in McCook. I remember him now, sitting near the front of the auditorium in a well-cut navy suit, all grave attention and sardonic eyes. He glances across the dusty street. "Interesting. Unexpected. They look so normal."

He is a University of Nebraska business graduate and a sub-scriber to the *New Yorker*, he tells me pointedly, handing over

his business card, which has a fax number on it. In response to
the theory that the land around us should go back to the buffalo,
Korell produces a low, eloquent snort.

"Give *Manhattan* back to the Indians, why don't you?" demands an indignant Wilma Christener, sixty-four, pausing on
her shopping rounds. It is not quite the non sequitur it sounds.
Where buffalo are, or may be, many residents of the Central
Plains instantly assume that Indians will be as well. The birth-
rate among Native Americans is soaring—a 19 percent increase
since 1980—and this statistic is brought up with great frequency
by white Plains dwellers.

"The Indians may be coming back, but in BMWs," says
Van Korell. He looks again at the Poppers, who stand in the
middle of the street talking to Ocia Weston. "They have no idea
of what ties us to this place." What does? I ask. They look at
each other.

"It's a fine place to raise kids," says Korell. "No air pollution,
no crime. Nice folks for the most part, neighbors you know and
can depend on. We've all been through a lot together, the last
few years, what with the drought and the failures and all."

Wilma Christener says, "You can wake up in the morning,
right in the middle of town, and hear the meadowlarks. *And* the
coyotes," she adds, triumphantly clinching the *argumentum ad
Hayes*.

A large crowd (by Hayes County standards) has gathered near
Johnny Scott's front door to watch the Poppers watch them. As
spectacle Frank and Deborah are a disappointment, or so mur-
mured comments suggest:

"I thought they'd be more, you know, colorful."

"They don't even have dark hair. Well, she does, sort of."

"They seem like nice plain folks."

"Certainly are dressed up."

Warm, too. Both Poppers look overheated and uncomfortable in their gray-wool speech outfits, donned for the dawn photo session, packed for this trip because the Weather Channel predicted a week of chill rain on the Plains. In sunwashed downtown Hayes Center the midmorning temperature is eighty-five and rising. Frank surveys the two dozen unsmiling onlookers (one filming him with a home video camera) and turns to his wife.

"What have we done," he inquires, "to the perfectly nice people of the Plains?"

"Alerted them," she replies. "And now no one is happy. Our next project may be safely overseas. Lithuanian housing reform sounds good."

They head over to introduce themselves, and after a moment of intense shyness on both sides there is a dam-burst of talk. Women crowd around Deborah to recount visits to a crowded, filthy, and expensive Manhattan; the men take Frank aside to explain that New York is the truly doomed American area, not the Plains. ("But I send my kids to their grandparents' back East every summer, so they can see traffic and black people," one man whispers to me.)

We break away to buy gleaming maroon strips of beef jerky and salted sunflower seeds. Both are popular snackfoods in Western states—the former a smoky-flavored descendant of the brine-soaked, air-dried buffalo meat that sustained Indians and hunters on the early Plains, the latter introduced by Russian settlers. Back in the car, Frank slumps in the passenger seat.

"So much for anonymous fieldwork. Everyone in this state knows us, and they're all mad. Why do they all have opinions about us? They've never even met us. I wish they didn't think I like New York. I *hate* the place, it's like the fall of Rome. Decadent. Aggressive. Humidified grime. I only go back there to visit my mother."

Van Korell taps on the window with an offer, gratefully received, to let the Poppers change clothes at his house, a substantial A-frame on the edge of town. The early eighties were awful, he says, sitting beside his enormous stone fireplace, elbows on knees. "For three years I didn't sleep. But troubles purified this place. The people who couldn't tough it out are gone. We're stabilizing now, or will be, if we can just get a little rain."

He stares out the window, then turns back, brightening. "Did I tell you that we do have one young farmer in the area? Just starting out, and doing pretty well so far."

Everywhere the Poppers go on the rural Plains, no matter how many farms and ranches have been lost to foreclosure, no matter how inexorable the small-town population decline, there always seems to be one young farmer somewhere in the vicinity, just starting out but doing pretty well so far, lovingly cited and anxiously watched by relatives and neighbors, a refuter of history, a stay against the inevitable, bread cast upon the waters, were there any waters to spare in these arid lands.

Jeffrey peels off in his rental car, heading to North Platte. He must catch the daily Denver plane, Federal Express his film to New York, and keep a doctor's appointment to renew his malaria, yellow fever, and dysentery shots. In four days he needs to be inside the People's Republic again, assigned to a two-month shoot near the Himalayas.

Equipped with directions from Wilma Christener (four miles out of town, left a mile to the creek bottom, *do not* cross the creek, ask at the first house to the east), Frank and Deborah and I head out to inspect the site of the buffalo hunt organized by General Philip Sheridan, Lieutenant General George A. Custer, and Nebraska's favorite son, Buffalo Bill Cody, for Grand Duke Alexis, third offspring of the Tsar of all the Russias.

In the mild January of 1872, courtiers in gold-laced uniforms drank champagne here and watched an enthusiastic war-dance by Spotted Tail and a hundred of his best Brule Sioux riders, but the elaborate tent encampment is only a brushwood depression in the prairie now, with a fine crop of wood ticks. The young duke was a poor shot, killing just two buffalo in two days of Hayes County hunting, but when his private railroad car reached Topeka there was a parade and banquet anyway, and the entire Kansas legislature recessed to see the fun.

Two years before Alexis's excursion, tanners in Germany, England, and Philadelphia had discovered that buffalo skin, properly treated with bug repellent before shipping, could be made into an unusually supple and handsome leather. This was very welcome news to the international leather trade, since Argentinian cowhide, badly overharvested, was becoming scarce, and no other reliable mass source had been discovered.

The prices offered were so fine by 1870s reckoning—$2.25 for the hide of a female buffalo, $3.25 for a bull—that thousands of buffalo runners (calling oneself a "buffalo hunter" was the mark of a tenderfoot) were soon out in search of the great herds, taking onto the Plains at least two mule-drawn skinning wagons, saddle horses trained to lie flat when the shooting began, and Sharps rifles equipped with telescopic sights and inch-and-a-quarter bullets. The one-man killing record, set in Kansas in the early 1870s, was 120 buffalo in forty minutes.

Three-quarters of a million buffalo hides went east on the railroads in 1873. So did thousands of buffalo hooves, to be polished into inkwells for curio shelves in Victorian parlors. So did thousands of barrels of delicacies: buffalo hams, cured in Dodge City; salted buffalo tongues; and fresh buffalo hump steaks, too, thanks to the new refrigerator cars. Before the Civil War between twenty and sixty million buffalo—no one, then or now, can be sure of the figure—roamed the Plains. In 1900 less than a thousand were alive.

As the world market for lean meat increases, many Western stockmen have begun to explore buffalo-raising with new seriousness. Some ranchers in Colorado and Wyoming now run over eight hundred head; in Montana there are commercial herds of a thousand and more. CNN mogul Ted Turner recently converted over 120,000 acres of his Montana lands from running cattle to running buffalo. ("They're better-looking," he explains.) In Benkelman, Nebraska—just over the time zone line into Mountain Standard, just shy of the Colorado border—the Poppers and I turn off to meet Robert Reichert's bison. Mr. Reichert, broad-bodied and ruddy after a lifetime in fields and barns, keeps twenty-four of the big-chested, black-maned animals on his forty-acre back lot: a hobby herd, really, though still impressive to New Jersey eyes.

"Thoreau was right: 'Eastward I go only by force; but westward I go free!' " Frank Popper shouts, standing joyously in the bed of the rancher's pickup. Deborah and I kneel by the wheel wells and hang on as we jolt across a rutted pasture, Colorado on our western horizon, Kansas to the south. A dozen shaggy brown buffalo press close beside the truck, keeping pace in a long easy gallop as the speedometer climbs to ten, fifteen, then twenty miles an hour.

An arm's length away, the great dark heads plunge, the black beards flow in the spring wind, and the small round eyes, chestnut-colored, roll and gleam. Even over the engine you can hear their breath burst out—*huff, huff, huff*—each time a one-ton body lands and rebounds. A dusty, spicy smell rises all around, part trampled pasture, part healthy ungulate. It is a fine, warm afternoon on the Great Plains, and they seem to enjoy the exercise.

Reichert spins the wheel, angling suddenly toward more buffalo standing farther up the field. They have been watching our impromptu stampede, unmoving but alert. He tries to herd the second cluster with the truck but they turn and scatter, seven enormous hindquarters bounding ahead of us, dense tawny rump fur shading to bay at the hocks. We stop, they stop, and our escort halts, too, with much stamping and blowing.

Three or four grunt to each other like hogs, and wander away. More stand into the wind, muzzles thrust forward, eyes half-closed, mouths open. Buffalo obtain much of their information by scenting, Reichert tells us; on open range they can smell water five miles off, and in winter find edible grass under twelve-inch snow.

All the heads have dropped earthward now, and we hear the steady rasp and rustle of pale-pink tongues against buffalo grass. One animal, a little smaller than his pasture-mates, stands always apart and grazes alone.

"See those white horns?" says Reichert. "That's a beefalo, half buffalo, half cow. The others shun him something awful." You can run three buffalo on the space required to maintain one domestic cow, Reichert says, watching his charges spread out across the field again. Buffalo have much sturdier constitutions, live longer—twenty-five to thirty years or more—and, not surprisingly, thrive better on the natural range fodder. Small steel identification tags sparkle and dangle in the furry ears, cow-fashion. (Modern grazing stock is frequently tagged, instead of branded.) He calls them like cows, too—"Suss! Suss! Soooo boss!" A few buffalo look up, tolerantly.

They really need more room to roam, but the neighbors fear that Reichert's buffalo might infect their cattle with brucellosis, an infectious disease that affects both species but is considerably more severe in cattle, sometimes causing cows to abort their calves. Brucellosis has been the cattleman's objection to commercial buffalo-raising since the turn of the century. Despite increasing veterinary evidence that these fears of disease transmission from buffalo to cattle are exaggerated, Reichert complies with his neighbors' wishes and keeps his buffalo fenced. I ask why definitive research on the problem has been so slow, and he laughs.

"Cattle will let you do anything you want. Ever try to take a blood sample from a buffalo? These are *wild* animals. Placid doesn't mean domesticated. They consent to remain here, and that's the bottom line."

The buffalo will remain shaggy till July, when their coats begin to shed. A few—he points them out—are already losing strips of pelt. These hang, matted like felt, from flanks and ribs. In high summer Reichert makes special trips out to this pasture to sprinkle flea powder in the wallows, because he hates to see the buffalo so miserable in the heat. Every winter he shoots some of them, five in a day. He lets the meat hang a while, "and then I turn them into little packages in the freezer. The others don't like it. They worry. You can *feel* them worrying."

I ask if buffalo-raising is profitable for him, and he laughs again. But his phone is always ringing. A Colorado insurance executive pleaded recently for permission to fly to Benkelman in a private jet to shoot one bull buffalo. Name any price. Reichert turned him down. Japanese investors and growers of beef have been talking to him about raising buffalo in Japan. School groups come out here a lot. To them he is Buffalo Bob.

Twenty yards away is a buffalo wallow. Two large young males sink to their knees, collapse with a thump into the shallow concavity in the bare earth, and conduct an ecstatic session of rolling and wriggling and good hard neck-scratching. But they come out of the wallow with their tails up; a bad sign, Reichert says. He is right. Heads low, horns clashing and locking, the animals charge, and charge again.

"I could live here," Frank Popper declares, eyes riveted on the tossing horns. "I could look at this land forever." Deborah nods but is not as convinced. Frank loves the deep prairie, America's steppes. She prefers edges and margins: eastern Montana, for instance, where the Plains change into something else before your eyes, rolling right to the foot of the Absaroka Range.

"The Plains permit no privacy, nothing to shelter under. They make you feel extraordinarily vulnerable," Deborah says, sitting braced on the hard edge of the pickup bed as we drive slowly back to the farmyard. She leans back to look at the ground flowing beneath the wheels, powdery and gray after three years of drought.

"We've thought of moving out here, a lot," says Frank, after a moment. He jumps out to open a gate for Reichert, then returns. The truck bumps on. "But what Great Plains university would have us? We'd be lynched before the first lecture. And think what Nicholas would go through in public school, poor guy. Like being the son of Bonnie and Clyde."

Though Reichert wants to get over to a livestock sale in northeast Nebraska and buy more buffalo (he is dressed up for the trip, in ironed jeans and crisp white shirt), he also wants to show us his latest acquisition, a dainty pedigreed Charolais cow, cream-colored from nose to tail. She is living at the moment in a private pen, a buffalo bull in the adjoining enclosure. They are smelling each other through the fence, somewhat cautiously to be sure, but Reichert is pleased.

He wants to breed Charolais and buffalo, hoping for a white calf. In Plains Indian tradition, among the Cheyenne, Mandan, Arapaho, and Pawnee, a white buffalo was thought to be favored by the gods, particularly the Sun God, and the women selected to clean and prepare the hide of a white buffalo underwent considerable ritual face-painting and prayer so that no harm would come to them or to the tribe. Blackfoot curing ceremonies and medicine bundles required a white buffalo robe to be hung outside the shaman's tipi, in the sunshine. If carried into battle, some Plains chiefs believed, such robes would shield the bearer from every harm.

"A lot of people would pay a lot of money for a white buffalo robe," Reichert says. He looks again at the prospective mother. "If this works, she's going to carry an awfully big calf. Might kill her. Might not. Have to try it, to find out."

As we drive west and away, the nineteen buffalo in the back pasture are galloping again, stocky, shaggy, prehistoric, as splendid as the bison on the cave walls at Lascaux.

North of Denver we meet a brief, violent cloudburst. As the downpour hammers at the windshield, I stick my hand out a passenger window, an incautious move. The temperature has dropped thirty degrees in as many minutes, and the great fat raindrops slam directly onto my palm like bursting water balloons. For half a mile we crawl along, headlights on, and then it is over. The fields on either side of the two-lane road lie soaked and steaming in the sudden late-afternoon sun. We crane around to watch the storm race south. The sky overhead darkens again—another black and gray and purple thunderhead, moving fast, raining as hard as it can—but precipitation in these parts does not always translate into wet ground. The prairie air is still so dry that great stripes of rain from the second storm hang suspended over the earth.

Fifteen years ago all these Colorado fields were cattle range, being grazed and sometimes overgrazed until another, quicker way to push the land to its limits gained ascendancy. The sodbusting of marginally arable acreage throughout the seventies and eighties, combined with immense investments of cheap water, migrant labor, and agricultural ingenuity, created from worn-out prairie marvelously organized miles of beans and sugar beets, planted fencepost-to-fencepost. Every field is painstakingly built up into low beds, edges neat as the corners on a hospital cot, to ensure efficient cultivation and harvesting, and in every bed the young plants rise in mathematically spaced phalanxes.

"What amazing country this is," says Frank Popper, hunched forward in the van seat to watch the two stormclouds sail past the front range of the Rockies. Above treeline the snowfields are brilliant against an indigo sky.

"I haven't seen this part of Colorado since the fifties. My parents brought my brother and me out here on what I now realize were Americanization trips," he adds. "We did a lot of those, the Grand Canyon, Navajo country, Yosemite."

Frank James Popper and Deborah Susan Epstein Popper met at Bailey's ice-cream shop in Harvard Square in 1967. He was a first-year graduate student in Harvard's Kennedy School of Government, sweating out Henry Kissinger's seminars in national security policy. They married when she was still a senior at Bryn Mawr.

Deborah is Manhattan-bred, a child of Washington Heights apartment houses, a scholarship student at New England boarding schools. Her Brooklyn-born father, Irving Epstein, was a University of Missouri graduate and a specialist in immigration law who died of a cerebral hemorrhage in 1953, leaving his widow to raise three daughters. Frank's father was an Austrian Jewish physician who fled the Nazis in 1938 on two hours' warning. Once in Chicago he married another Viennese and managed to get their parents to America just before the war began. He remained in Chicago to conduct pathology research at Cook County Hospital and raise two sons. In 1965 the elder Dr. Popper helped found Mount Sinai Hospital's medical school in New York, becoming the school's dean and president in 1972. He died in 1988. While Frank Popper was growing up, both German and English were spoken in the house. When he is very tired, or very frustrated, the German accent of his childhood returns to his voice.

"I loved that whole Saul Bellow world," Frank says now, watching the Rockies rise and rise before us out of the golden prairie, "that Irish-German-Jewish-Italian-immigrant Chicago where class boundaries change almost house by house, and you may be Jewish but you know all the saints' days anyway. My father was so deeply a European that he could never fully Americanize. But he wanted me to. So I tried to understand the culture completely. To scout out the territory. To pioneer."

From my downtown Denver hotel window I can see a sliver of the mountains still. They look discolored and yellowish; urban air quality this week in the Queen City is rated low to unacceptable. My mountain vista is obscured as well by three glass-sheathed office towers. Whole floors, I notice, stand unoccupied.

I also notice the upcoming-events page in the complimentary

room copy of *Denver Magazine*: "Two eastern professors who propose that Denver and the Great Plains should be emptied of people so the deer and the antelope can play will be here to pay their last respects. . . . The Poppers will obviously get paid to play at the National Planning Conference. . . . It's likely that more than a few will have buffalo chips to throw. . . . For locals planning to stay in Denver, the Poppers have attained a status once reserved for horse thieves. 'Depopulation of the Great Plains? This is crap,' suggests one local planner."

The room phone rings. "Did you see that story? Oh, *Christ!*" cries Frank, in an agonized howl.

Two hours later, Deborah and Frank stand back-to-back at a meet-the-Poppers reception sponsored by the Center for the New West, a Denver organization defined by its executive director, Philip Burgess, as a think tank devoted to Western economic policy and growth. In Burgess's suburban condominium, the living room, dining room, kitchen, library, and deck are crowded with lawyers and bureaucrats, Hermés scarves and polished cowboy boots, third helpings of Cabernet Sauvignon and scallion beef. Frank and Deborah are smiling gamely, shaking hand after hand, but a number of the wide smiles issued in return are purely social.

I intercept Joseph Luther, assistant dean of the University of Nebraska architecture school, who is to debate Frank Popper at the American Planning Association convention the next morning. Luther, a Vietnam veteran who received his doctorate from Texas A&M, is plump and bearded, wearing a natty beige linen jacket. I ask Dean Luther's opinion on the Buffalo Commons. Dean Luther dislikes mythic visions.

"Out here we believe in maintaining a very positive attitude of thinking," he explains, lowering himself onto a comfortably overstuffed couch in the Burgess library. A caterer's assistant moves in quickly with a silver tray of cherry tomatoes topped with smoked-salmon mousse and sprigs of dill, but Luther waves him off.

"Why, if global warming comes, we'll just plant palm trees and make Omaha the next Sunbelt. Frank Popper represents Europe, the East, Harvard, federal interference—everything the good people of the Plains want to get away from. And, of course, there *is* the anti-Semitic thing, which is real unfortunate. No, we will fight the Poppers, all the way."

To encourage its study of economic development in states beyond the Mississippi, the Center for the New West receives corporate funding from a variety of sources. One is US West, the AT&T successor in many Western states, whose international interests range from Hong Kong cable TV to Hungary's cellular-phone system. Other supporters of the Center for the New West are the Manhattan-based investment banking firm of Goldman Sachs; the national accounting firm of Coopers & Lybrand; and the Denver law firm of Davis Graham & Stubbs. The Center's board of directors includes Senator Dennis DeConcini of Arizona and the Poppers' old acquaintance Governor George Sinner of North Dakota.

The Center for the New West predicts that the twenty-first-century Plains will resemble an urban archipelago, its population islands linked by a service economy. Its picture of the Plains to come is an updated, high-tech version of Walter Prescott Webb's conception of the American West as an oasis civilization. Through press releases, media lunches, opinion columns, and op-ed pieces, in position papers and newsletters and reports and studies and conference proceedings, the Center and its sponsors attempt to market their view of a region's future.

That vision has no place for a Buffalo Commons, and no patience with the powerfully romantic past the Poppers have invoked. The whole Buffalo Commons controversy, from the New West point of view, resembles a low, spinning, unwelcome fastball, all the way from Middlesex County, New Jersey. The New Westers wish the Poppers would get off the Plains, and stick to LULUs.

Phil Burgess, small, many-chinned, and balding, leads me onto the deck of his condo and gestures at its backyard view: the lights of dozens of high rises and office towers along the Denver-Littleton freeway. "As you see, remarkably few buffalo are roaming Denver," he observes. Denver lies at the edge of the Plains, not on them; its population has risen 200 percent in the last thirty years.

"And frankly," Phil Burgess continues, "we prefer solid development to fantasy. The Poppers mistake change for decline. We at the Center are presently bifurcating our efforts, and concentrating on the I-5 interstate corridor—i.e., San Diego to Seattle—as a problem apart from rural development, but many of the same recommendations and conclusions apply. The future of the Great Plains is in its cities and towns."

What about the small towns and the rural areas? I ask.

A flicker of extreme annoyance, beautifully controlled. "What *about* them? There are a great many opportunities in the New West economy for such residents," Burgess says briskly. "Home-based telemarketing. Computer programming. Dude ranches."

I try to imagine retraining Ocia Weston, Wilma Christener, Van Korell, Johnny Scott—or Paul Ornan—in these pursuits.

Burgess's original credentials are solidly Eastern: raised in Lebanon, Pennsylvania, a Ph.D. from American University in Washington, D.C., a stretch as a tenured professor of political science (specializing in international relations) at Ohio State University. His early researches focused on Norway. But he works hard for his adopted region, a punishing schedule of keynote speeches, addresses to business groups, and panel presentations at economic-development seminars.

Standing on the deck of his condo this soft summer night, watching the mountain sky deepen to violet and a pale crescent moon emerge over the office parks of exurban Denver, Burgess is very much on duty. He speaks, over the party noise, almost entirely in the phraseology of his own newsletters and advertorials: The New Economy. The Ongoing Story of America's Transformation. The Negative, Handwringing Commentaries That Undermine Investor Confidence in Companies That Obtain a Large Part of Their Revenues from This Region.

Behind us rises a sudden roar of laughter. Real-estate developers, sharing war stories: ". . . like the time I rented a 727 for the day to run those Japanese through Austin *and* Houston *and* San Jose? Five industrial sites in nine hours, oh, man, a personal best."

Patricia Nelson Limerick is on the sofa in the library, picking bits of onion from cold rotini salad tossed in a black olive–red pepper vinaigrette, her round face discontented. A Yale Ph.D., she taught at Harvard and is now a star of the history department at the University of Colorado–Boulder and a board member of the Center for the New West.

She does not like Frederick Jackson Turner, she tells me ("Turner is closer to poetry than historical reality") and does not like those who ignore the moral complexities of the West. History as heroism, as a triumph of intrepid courage against extraordinary odds, is to Limerick a distorted pattern for understanding this American region. She sees instead a legacy of conquest and its many disagreeable consequences: white male adventurism, racism, greed, environmental stupidity.

Most of the big nineteenth-century issues are still with us, Limerick points out—water rights, land management, border control. Her face brightens as she talks about language and its uses when practicing revisionist history. "Frontier" in Europe, for instance, meant a defended border, but here it denoted vacancy and opportunity—"Associations that use you before you use them. I prefer 'borderlands,' just as I choose 'encounter' over 'discovery' to describe the first European contacts with this continent. It never hurts to encourage linguistic neurosis in Western specialists."

She wanders toward the dining room, where Phil Burgess and the Poppers have reached a temporary stalemate regarding their competing visions of the Plains that are to come. Their exchanges have been reduced to sign language plus verbal italics. "*Urban-archipelago society*," Burgess insists, acting it out with his hands, plop, plop, plop, Laramie, Wichita, Abilene. "*Oceans of land in between*," Frank counters, as Deborah makes helpful waving motions to indicate large expanses of shortgrass prairie.

At the Denver Convention Center, almost from the moment the doors open for registration, the thirteenth annual meeting of the American Planning Association is running on nerves. APA members who work within the academy, teaching in the nation's eighty-odd accredited graduate programs of urban and regional planning, can be as high-strung as tenors and inclined toward the messianic. (Assistant professor from Berkeley to a graduate student from Tufts, while waiting in the food-concession line: "I can save America! Why does no one listen!") Academic planners sometimes like to say that they are paid to have visions, to be decoders of place.

The makers of place are found in the profession's much larger pragmatic wing, those planners who spend their nights in zoning meetings and their days in sewage-district arbitration. No less vocal, they are especially impatient with theory, and with academics who suggest that they are sellouts, incapable of macro-thinking. Practitioners thrive on tradeoffs, compromises, bargainings, deals.

The struggle for ascendance between these two impulses permeates every session and every topic, from restructuring town boards and legislating private waste disposal to trends in roadside oceanfront sign regulation and development-agreement drafting techniques. Whatever the intellectual politics involved, no one falls asleep in APA sessions; quite the contrary. The lecture halls and conference rooms are a panoply of tics and twitches. Planners discussing planning bite pencils, twirl hair, fold and shred the handouts, doodle fiercely, chomp gum and Gelusil. And no wonder; urban and regional planners are hired by consulting firms, by developers, and by cities and counties and states and the federal government with very specific and completely contradictory mandates: they are to protect the environment, save the cities, and develop jobs, all at the same time.

Sunk in the low-backed armchairs that dot the central atrium's floor, ignoring the roar of chat that rises in this high-ceilinged public space as planners with briefcases and planners in work boots hurry along the crosswalks and up the escalators, conventioneers of all persuasions hold forth to me on the Buffalo Commons. Few, whether theorists or pragmatists, interpret the Poppers' proposal as a literal solution to Plains difficulties. All regard Frank (and Deborah, though she is a geographer and not a planner) as redefiners of the policy landscape, idealistic mavericks with an unusual practical bent.

The Poppers are also perceived as dangerous. They are too far ahead of their time, many peers feel. In an age of compromise and distancing, they appear to be playing for real. This can be scary. One St. Louis planner likens their ideas to the act of asking, circa 1910, that separate drinking fountains for whites and blacks be abolished across the South.

I talk to a Marxist planner from the Midwest who sees nothing wrong with loosing the Poppers onto the Plains. The planning profession is debating its role in society a great deal these days, and he is glad they are aiding and abetting. To him the Poppers are applied utopianists, faithful to the profession's original urge to be out and about, helping society—an impulse that seems to be fading now, as the think tank model moves to the fore.

"A lot of us don't go outdoors at all these days. It's so risky and sweaty," he says, burlesquing a dainty moue. "But I'd be happier with the Poppers' work if I knew for sure they'd read all the contemporary studies, like the new literature on ethnic derivations of landholdings. People with Yankee ancestry, say, are much more prone to see land as a production resource, and more willing to dispose of it and acquire another parcel somewhere else. German-Americans see land as a generational legacy and will do almost anything to hang on. It's not enough to affirm that farmers are leaving. I want to know who's leaving and why."

Phil Burgess, a flying wedge of Center for the New West personnel at his back, crosses the lobby, and the Marxist professor watches him go, looking thoughtful. He knows Burgess by sight, though they have never spoken; planning as a profession is still small enough to operate under South Dakota rules. Burgess's attitude toward the problem of the Plains, the Midwesterner observes, is very Marxist, though Burgess would faint to hear it so described: the conviction that capital conquers all—time and space and place. "Don't use my name," the Marxist says, by way of farewell. "I'm up for tenure next year."

A substantial minority of planners, and many others with an interest in Western development, believe that the Poppers are advocating evacuation and/or triage for the Plains. One persistent roadblock in the Poppers' path has been the need to explain, repeatedly, that depopulation does not equal evacuation. Another is the need to explain, also repeatedly, that triage is the intellectual property of Mark Lapping, who by a quirk of research timing is now known from Texas to Montana as "that other Rutgers professor."

Lapping (a Finnish-Jewish Vermont farmboy once described as possessing "the personality of Hamlet in Falstaff's body") is a Rutgers dean who at forty-five has already founded two major schools of planning, one at the University of Guelph in Ontario, one at Kansas State, and has coauthored the standard textbook on American rural planning. Lapping's investigations in rural Kansas led him to conclude, reluctantly, that federal and state resources may have to be withdrawn from towns and farm areas that are clearly failing, in order to concentrate already-scarce funds on rural locales that still have a chance. He calls the plan "triage," mindful of the medical term employed on World War I battlefields by French army doctors forced to decide which injured soldiers to treat, the most gravely wounded generally given the least aid on the expectation they would expire despite all help.

Where do you fall in the spectrum of Plains planning? I ask Lapping, as we sit in the convention center's lobby. He traces an arc in the air and begins chopping off segments, left to right. Triage is clearly the most drastic solution so far, he says cheerfully; followed by the Poppers' Buffalo Commons; and then Wes Jackson's work on developing sustainable, Plains-friendly agriculture at the Land Institute in Salina, Kansas. Then come the less long-term, less interventionist solutions: the Center for the

New West's salvation through economic adaptation, and finally the loose collection of agencies and private firms that currently run training sessions in economic self-help and leadership development for small-town business owners and elected officials not willing to accept as inevitable the severe declines forecast for the rural Plains by outside academics like Lapping and the Poppers.

"I did a lot of people-development work in Kansas, and it was rough," Lapping tells me. "The Plains have, shall we say, a deep disinclination to be disturbed. Hear no evil, speak no evil! At Kansas State I kept getting, 'Now, Mark, let's not have any negativity.' In New Jersey you run up against the arrogance of power, the three-thousand-miles-of-nothing-out-there-why-bother mindset." He leans back in his chair, looking cheerful no longer, only tired; an administrator who has seen too much stubborn ignorance on both sides of the 98th meridian.

"Frank and Deborah are quietly—well, maybe not *quietly*—trying to wake up a region by democratizing information, and high time. We need to figure out ways for the Plains to sustain and survive. *Fast*. There's not much groundwater left in the Ogallala aquifer, you know."

I talk to Dan Lauber, a former president of the American Planning Association, a planner and land-use attorney from Chicago known in the field for his political savvy. Asked about the Poppers and the Buffalo Commons, he groans.

"Frank and Deborah always research something to death, then announce their findings too honestly. It's a terrible flaw. They're so damn guileless. They've uncovered something that scares the influential moneymakers, and both of them go wandering through the very corrupt world of planning and development saying innovative stuff no one wants to hear. It's a pity the response is not logic so much as an emotional striking-back.

Messenger-killing. Frank has also *got* to stand still when he talks and stop making weird faces when he thinks."

The Joe Luther–Frank Popper debate on the future of the Great Plains packs a convention center hall with city managers, zoning experts, planning professors, preservationists, and development commissioners eager to argue, eager to watch. The Poppers have become planning celebrities, very nearly a contradiction in terms. Joe Luther, a highly visible member of the Western Planners Association, is the homeboy favorite with the many trans-Mississippi planners present.

The edges of the long meeting room are cluttered with the lights and cables of television crews, some sent by local stations, one privately imported by Luther. Deborah sits in the last row, just under the camera of the Denver CBS affiliate, ready to make coaching notes on rhetoric and strategy. The New West contingent marches in, claiming chairs near the back on the other side of the aisle. Deborah waves. They look toward her—a seated and unsmiling Burgess bows from the waist—then look away, almost as one.

Joe Luther proves a practiced orator, highly photogenic (I check in a nearby monitor) and given to measured William Jennings Bryan gestures. He plays to the cameras, the permanent record always in mind, whereas Frank Popper earnestly tries to convince the house. Frank is faster and funnier than Luther in repartee but often forgets to speak in sound bites.

Frank attempts to explain the characteristics of the Plains as defined in the Popper research design. Joe Luther waits impatiently for him to finish, then pounces.

"So we should rip out the whole area from our maps and label it 'Death?' We hear a scream here and a scream there as Frank's pencil drives through our towns," cries Luther, arms wide. "Grind triage under your heel!" he implores the crowd.

"That's not us, that's Mark Lapping, the other Rutgers person," says Frank, but Luther keeps going.

"Let us not be buffaloed!"

"Get Popper's reaction," the local television reporter hisses to her cameraman. Deborah winces, but for once her husband wears no odd thinker's expression. He sits still, looking politely bored, a perfect faculty-meeting face. He is learning.

"If the Plains are such a wonderful place, why do so many people leave?" Frank demands. "The Plains have developed a tidy rationale for this: 'We produce great people.' If this keeps up, the Great Plains' major export crop will be its young."

"Well, you can't understand the Plains," says Luther, in a fine throbbing baritone, "unless you've sat down with its people in a grange hall, as I have, and shared their hopes, yes, and their dreams."

"We are not out to depopulate Denver. Or Dallas, or Billings," Frank snaps, after yet another charge of plotting Plains evacuation. "All those places lie well away from areas affected by a Buffalo Commons. We're talking free-market, gradual, generations-long change. All of us can recognize it's happening and talk frankly about the options for the rural Plains, or we can turn away our faces and the buffalo really will come back."

People in the audience are testifying with passion now, denouncing the Commons, inviting the Poppers to visit Bozeman and witness its economic health ("Bozeman isn't on the Plains either," Deborah says under her breath), calling out that they feel themselves as good as any Easterner, and harder-working, too.

Deborah, beside me, mutters, "I can't stand this," and leaps to her feet. She pushes her glasses up her nose and hugs a gray paisley shawl to her shoulders.

"That's not what the Buffalo Commons is saying," she calls

out. Throughout the room, people quiet to listen, those in the front turning in their chairs to see her better. All the cameras swing in Deborah's direction.

"The Buffalo Commons is saying, 'Let's expand our options, let's try a variety of things in areas where, historically, *nothing* has worked.' There are many ways to keep your pride and use your resources and survive. Don't throw away new information just because it's new. Be flexible, for heaven's sake. I'm a geographer, not a planner, but I thought that was what you people did. Plan." On the dais, Frank is grinning proudly.

The session has run overtime; the room must be cleared. The Center for the New West contingent stalks out. One of their Colorado sympathizers pushes through the crowd of departing planners. His face is nearly as maroon as beef jerky, so suffused that I fear he is about to have a stroke.

He hisses at Deborah, "*Who's paying you to do this?*" She stares him down.

Frank Popper stays angry all the way home. Looking out the plane window over western Nebraska, where McCook and the Republican River are just visible through broken clouds, he says, "We were being used, forty-seven ways." Over Springfield, Illinois, he announces, "I'm sick of being reviled as a heartless, overeducated Eastern fool. Especially since I'm from Chicago." Over Dayton, Ohio: "And I'm not crazy about getting up to explain research knowing almost everyone in the room hates you and deliberately won't listen anyway."

By Newark he has calmed down. "Only amateurs stay mad."

In the next weeks the Poppers' mailbox at Rutgers fills and refills with newspaper clippings.

The *Denver Post*, on the Frank Popper–Joe Luther debate:

. . . Noting that Potter had suggested the Plains be abandoned in the face of global warming, Luther suggested that perhaps New Jersey, or California, should also be abandoned because continued warming would endanger the nation's shorelines. Potter branded that suggestion "completely illegitimate" and members of the audience joined in the verbal fray.

Although they spoke animatedly for 90 minutes, Potter didn't put a probability index on his buffalo homeland and Luther didn't provide any clear alternatives, saying, "The action plan to achieve a substantial society on the Great Plains would take another hour to explain."

From the director of the Center for Great Plains Studies at the University of Nebraska, writing in the Omaha *World-Herald*:

It really should be called the Buffalo Bill Commons Wild West Show. This is a degrading proposal for Native Americans and all other Plains residents. We, in short, are the zoo.

The McCook *Daily Gazette*, McCook, Nebraska:

We felt that most of the Popper's arguments for what they see as the demise of the Great Plains as we know it were adequately shot down. One has to give the Poppers credit for courage though, facing an almost totally hostile audience made even more so by a hot auditorium. The question is, what now?

I head back to Princeton to finish up my teaching for the year, trying to keep the freshmen attending to Henry James and Kate Chopin even as sunlight and the smell of mown grass drift through the high arched windows of our classroom.

On the last day of the semester I give a pop geography quiz to the eighteen students in my American literature discussion section. The demands are not excessive—on a blank map of the

United States, identify each state and name its capital. The big square states baffle most of them utterly. One kid from Maryland gets nothing right west of the Missouri, not even California. I ask him how he gets around; he explains that he boards the airplane, eats lunch, and five hours later he's somewhere else, no problem.

A boy from Denton, Texas, agrees, adding that he always knows he's reached friendly country if cattle are grazing by the runway. He can identify nothing east of St. Louis. I ask him where he is now, and he points to Connecticut. I look at him.

"Why should I care?" he says, meaning it. "I hate it out here. I'm going home when I graduate, and I'm never coming out again."

Checking the rest of the impromptu map readings, I learn some new state capitals. Juno, Alaska; Lansing, South Dakota; Frankfurter, Kentucky. Still, when filling out 1980 U.S. Census forms, a quarter-million people in the Plains states carefully blackened the self-identification box for "Central American." I decide not to give grades on the quiz.

Later, I walk beneath Princeton's Gothic towers, leaning hard against a tide of people, more bodies packed onto a campus twelve blocks long than in all of Hayes County, Nebraska. In honor of graduation and reunions week, and in honor of summer, a student environmental group is giving a public reading in the library plaza. Above the academic chat and the shouts of middle-aged alumni in tiger hats, I am startled to hear again Black Elk's lament for the Plains.

"To the center of the world you have taken me," an earnest boy in denims declaims to the passing crowds, "and shown me the power and endurance of the bison, the beauty and strangeness of the earth, the power to make live and to destroy." I glance around, but no one seems to be listening.

86

III
NO MAN'S
LAND

THE SOUTHERN PLAINS:
Oklahoma
and Texas

A T 7:00 P.M. on a Thursday in November, five months later, a cold night wind smelling of wet sagebrush rolls through the open glass doors of the Oklahoma City Sheraton. It brushes against the Tulsa accountants arguing barbecue secrets by the elevators; wells over the professional riders, arms filled with girths and braided quirts, talking barrel racing beside the potted palms. As the wind moves through, I see guests all over the lobby pause in mid-syllable and raise their heads—the profoundly Plains gesture, serious and unself-conscious, of a citizenry still able to read the scent of rain.

The wild pure gust of prairie night has entered the Sheraton because the three hundred guests of the dinner lecture hosted by the Oklahoma Academy for State Goals all seem to be arriving in one jostling phalanx. Seen from the first turning of the lobby stair, their progress is easy to track, a river of color among the neat brown polyester backs of the lesser conventioneers.

I stand to one side and watch the splendid dinner dresses go by. Strapless magenta, with violently nipped-in waist. A waterfall of electric-blue flounces, and another of red. Sleeves beaded in crystal and jet. Heels so recklessly cantilevered that some women ascend to the Plaza Ballroom by hoisting themselves hand over hand along the banister, then seizing, at the summit, an indulgent male elbow. Others flourish minks and sables ahead of them like matador capes to keep poufed skirts from danger in the crush. One, sixtyish, with a leathery ranchwoman's face, straight-arms a mink coat *and* a sable stole, earning respectful glances, and all the maneuvering room she wants.

The talk is of ice, which seems to universally terrify:

"Do y'all think it'll ice?"

"I'm real scared of ice."

"It better not ice, or I'll just die."

Settling down to dinner takes several minutes. Up and down the long, hot room, over the drone of formal thank-yous to sponsors being read out from the dais—Conoco, Grace Petroleum, Phillips Petroleum, Oklahoma Natural Gas Company, Kerr McGee, Sooner Pipe and Supply, BancOklahoma, First National Bank of Broken Arrow—many of the men continue to shoulder-slap, right and left, right and left, crying "Harvey!" "Merle!" "Duwayne!"

The banquet room fills with the clash of metal chair legs. Many of the women guests are moving closer to each other, creating congenial huddles.

"Isn't this cozy?" says a pleased realtor from Pawhuska.

Conditions in the Sheraton banquet hall tonight are close, but they are not cozy, not where the Poppers are concerned. The Oklahoma Academy has a distinguished history in state public affairs—it opposed segregation when such stands were less than popular—but the current members seem to want nothing to do with a Buffalo Commons.

"I *dressed* tonight, to show those Eastern professors what's what," announces a fortyish woman in knuckle-to-knuckle diamonds to her oilman tablemate, resplendent in gilded ostrich-leather cowboy boots. He pats her shoulder approvingly.

"I'm already so mad at these two, I could just spit," adds a development-commission director on his other side. She gets patted too.

At the podium, Frank Popper is working his way through a series of overheads displaying land-use projections for the Southern Plains. He is trying not to squint in the blaze of arc lights trained on him by the camera crews from ABC's "World News Tonight," NBC's "Today Show," and Rutgers' television unit, trying not to peer at his seven-foot image turning and gesturing on the three enormous screens in the corners of the packed room, trying not to provoke the Oklahoma Academy for State Goals to riot before dessert.

The press has been told to spread out along the back of the hall, and with practiced speed, battered metal equipment trunks and strong vinyl-net bags of videotape have materialized from the hallway outside. I pull a chair near two tables of Academicians, all enthusiastic talkers. Between bobbing heads I glimpse Barry Serafin of ABC News, standing slump-shouldered beside his Houston-based crew, squinting at shots in the viewfinder.

All the network people are nearly gray with exhaustion. At lunchtime today they were still in Burbank, Washington, Chicago, New York. Four full camera crews and a dozen newspaper reporters and magazine writers make the edges of the room a chaos of cables and lights and tote bags. Producers urgently confer on shots and logistics, print journalists flip notebook pages and fiddle with voice-activated recorders.

Jeffrey Aaronson's photograph of Frank and Deborah and their attaché cases atop a Hayes County haybale—a splash of golden grasses and blue Nebraska sky across two pages of the *New York Times Magazine*—has not helped the Poppers' anonymity quotient. Over the summer the Commons has become a hot media item, especially in Europe. There the Plains are not flyover country, but a landscape of marvels. Anything tied to the Wild West sells in Germany and England and France. *Figaro* and *Der Stern* and the *Economist* are assigning stories on the plight of the Plains. So are *Time* and *Esquire*. The BBC wants to film the Poppers. So does a California educational-video company, and Italian national TV.

Frank and Deborah have been lecturing and chairing throughout the Rutgers summer term, as well as crunching numbers on the Proteus computers, answering hundreds of Commons-related letters, and fielding ceaseless, baffling calls from editors and producers. ("When are you two heading for buffaloland? We have a crew free this week," Connie Chung's office announced. Then: *"November? That's* three months away!" Three months is forever, in television. But the new semester starts in September, explained Frank; we have to set up our courses; we have to get our daughter off to college; we have to paint the house. The voice from 57th Street did not call back.)

Now November is here, and across the table at the Academy for State Goals dinner a very fat banker from Anadarko waves for the Pawhuska realtor's attention. "Look at Walter," he advises, one gold tooth gleaming.

Imported from Washington, D.C., to oppose the Poppers, Walter Hill (Assistant Undersecretary of Agriculture for Small Community and Rural Development, former minority leader in the Oklahoma House of Representatives, B.S. in agronomy, Panhandle State, M.S. and Ph.D. in soil science, Oklahoma State) has claimed the dais seat farthest from Frank and Deborah. He is speed-reading a set of photocopied articles on the Buffalo Commons under cover of the tablecloth. He flips pages with one hand and worries with the other at a sodden gray slice of roast buffalo, the banquet's main course. Undersecretary Hill chews, and chews, and attacks the mixed vegetables.

"A variety of statistical indicators show a constant and discouraging downward trend," intones Frank Popper from the lectern, "all occurring past the rainfall line of the 98th meridian."

"We call it Highway Eighty-one," whispers a sharp-nosed woman in pink chiffon.

"In the 1890s the Plains were treated to the alarming sight of fully loaded wagon trains heading out of the Plains and going east," Frank continues.

The Lawton oilman snaps his Rolex band dismissively. "He knows his history, but he don't know us." The man from Anadarko mimics a massive snore.

Deborah slips another transparency onto the screen. It shows Oklahoma counties in distress, and the difficulty indicators cover nearly half the area of the state between the 98th meridian and the eastern edge of the Panhandle.

The woman in pink is galvanized into sudden attention.

"That's my mama's country there, Ellis County! They want to close my old county down!"

She stares first at the crosshatched areas on the map, then at the oilman, alarmed. He looks away.

"The fences will vanish, the grasslands return," Frank says, grasping the walnut-stained plywood podium and rocking his upper body back and forth, enunciating slowly, pausing between phrases now.

"In another generation, two at the most, the Plains as we know them will be remarkably changed. It is already changing. The preliminary 1990 Census returns show the Plains population dropping far faster than anyone expected, including us."

Another Oklahoma map goes up, and another. The angry joshing turns to stony gazes and sucked-in cheeks as Deborah moves to the lectern to take over the commentary.

"If current economic, population, and ecological trends continue," Deborah tells them firmly, "—not accelerate, just continue—we can project a Great Plains that looks very much like *this*."

At the sight of the 110 counties of the Buffalo Commons, a spreading bloom on the map like a red algae tide, the room goes instantly and utterly silent, so silent that the whir of the small cooling fan inside Deborah's overhead projector and a soft-clicking relay in one of the television lights are suddenly the loudest sounds there. At every table men and women lean forward, listening hard, for once not looking about them to gauge group reaction. It is suddenly a room of private terrors, not noisy denials, as Oklahoma's confident constant raucous talk deflates and vanishes and in its place is echoed the dreadful hush of McCook and Denver, as the Popper version of the future sinks in, and is processed, and the stomach lurches, and the bank overdraft is considered, and considered again, in horrid instant replay. The Lawton oilman scribbles a three-word note on his program and passes it to the Anadarko banker, who nods, un-smiling. I retrieve the piece of paper later; it reads: "Buy grass-seed stock."

"The Plains are not homogenous. North Dakota is in far worse trouble than Oklahoma, where the Panhandle is doing quite well," Deborah notes, indicating on the overhead map the long thin expanse of western Oklahoma. "And your minerals exploration is increasingly efficient, taking over from cattle ranching. Just in time, because by 1989, Florida, Kentucky, and Tennessee each produced more beef cattle than did nine states in the American West. But oil and gas prosperity—like live-stock, like the water-intensive crops such as cotton and alfalfa grown all over this state—is almost completely dependent, as elsewhere across the southern half of the Plains, on the rapidly depleting Ogallala aquifer."

"What's that?" the Anadarko man's wife asks him anxiously. He stares at the screen. She shakes his arm, fiercely. *"What's that?"*

"The water table, I think," he says slowly. "Never heard it called that before."

Above them, on the great map of the Plains, Deborah's silhouetted hand traces the aquifer's reach. It is an egg-shaped area, seven hundred miles long, four hundred wide, reaching from upper Texas beyond the banks of the Platte River in central Nebraska, then slipping west to underlie the dry reaches of eastern Colorado and Wyoming. Under her relentless finger the oval shrinks, and shrinks again, to show the ongoing retreat of the Plains' main water source.

Deborah turns over her last page and tries to smile at her motionless listeners.

"Our vision of the Plains is that of one of the greatest American poets, Walt Whitman, who wrote after a journey to California and back, 'The Plains, while less stunning at first sight, last longer, fill the esthetic sense fuller, precede all the rest and make North America's characteristic landscape.' Please remember that when he wrote those words, he, too, was living in New Jersey."

Four people laugh. Undersecretary Hill stands for the rebuttal, stiff-shouldered and reluctant in a black suit. The photosensitive lenses of his rectangular metal-framed eyeglasses mistake the television lights for a tropical noon and immediately turn dark gray.

The crowd perks up. Ready to cheer one of their own, I assume, but Oklahoma surprises me once more. Each Hill pronouncement brings loud commentary from the hall—not a revival's call-and-response, but the one-way editorializing of people who habitually talk back to their TV sets.

Hill says, "My daddy homesteaded right near Beaver Creek"—"Damn right!" comes a voice from the crowd—"and I believe the private sector is a better steward of the land than any federal government!"

("Bud's giving the wrong speech. Again," comments a balding dinner guest at the table to my left.)

"There's always been distance in rural counties," Hill continues. "It takes a long time to get places, sometimes. And sparsity. Sparsity is big on the Plains. In rural areas, there's very few people around."

(Lawton man, two feet away from me: "No, really?")

"Things like health care cost more. But health care is important to survive."

(Anadarko man: "So we'll have first-aid stations. Get to the point.")

"Oklahoma folks know all about hard times, and they're still the best, hardest-workingest folks in the world. That ought to count for *something*."

("Sit down and let someone else take them on!")

When Hill is gently ushered back to his seat, Frank and Deborah rise to take questions, but without much more apparent success at winning hearts and minds. At the very first query—"What's the benefit to all this? Do you two profit somewhere along the line?"—Deborah eyes her husband's bulging neck veins, then neatly intercepts the microphone.

("Good," says the woman in pink with deep satisfaction,

draining her wineglass. "She's not going to let him talk. Tell 'em, girl.")

The questions rumble on. Most are perorations, stylized and boosteristic, constructed to earn points with peers around the room.

We have the best damn wheat economy in the United States; are you going to ignore Oklahoma's feed grain output?

Just let big business invest here for a change and not in Texas or Colorado, build some factories, we'll show everyone Oklahomans can work.

Say it straight: Your Buffalo Commons means more government interference. Get food prices up, and more farmers would stay on the land.

You New Jersey urban people can't understand; we always have hard times. Always. They come and go; bad cycles, hard times, dry months, dry years.

"Try dry decades," barks Frank, finally. "Listen: You cannot go on as you are. Ignoring a shift this fundamental is regional suicide."

("The bastard," says the Anadarko banker, frowning. "I thought he was gonna talk on buffalo. This is all about economics.")

The camera crews converge on the platform to record the after-talk arguments, of which there are many. Frank and Deborah are ringed by Betacams; sound technicians lean over, crawl under, climb onto the head table, shielding microphones from the clatter of a thousand dishes being cleared away. No one asks to interview Walter Hill.

A lot of Academicians want to give the Poppers a piece of their mind, or have their picture taken with them, or both. ("I feel like Mount Rushmore," Frank mutters.) Mr. and

Mrs. Howard have come 360 miles from Tahlequah for this moment and hand me their small box camera to do the honors. They beam into the lens, arms around Deborah, who looks patient, and Frank, who does not. Scott Swearingen, a business consultant from Tulsa, stands at my shoulder and watches the Poppers carefully, scanning their faces over and over as if searching for some hidden malice, some concealed intent.

"Hill didn't refute them," he says softly, repeatedly. "He didn't refute them. Not one bit. We don't have the language for what they're trying to tell us."

Nearly an hour after the presentation's close at least a hundred dinnergoers remain, huddling together now as if for warmth. Janet Drummond, of Pohaska, watches the queue of questioners continue to push toward the dais and its pool of light and heat and noise.

"Those two are right, in a way," she observes in an even voice. "We don't want to give up what we have. What little we have. It's just—"

Among her half-dozen listeners a silence falls, filled with the clatter and tinkle of banquet teardown. She tries again.

"These Easterners, coming in here, saying, 'The land is all of ours. One nation.' We're not used to thinking that way, is all."

Beside her, the Academy's president and chair of the First Oklahoma Corporation, James Tolbert III, moves restlessly.

"I know. I'm a cattle rancher," he says to her, half to comfort, half to endorse. "It goes against everything I ever knew. Ever believed. Regardless, we should listen." He looks around the circle, his face fierce. "This is *gorgeous* country."

All look down at their exquisitely polished shoes, then drift away with nods but no farewells. West of Minneapolis, no one ever says good-bye.

In 1889 the first Oklahoma Land Rush went right over what is now downtown Oklahoma City, a tight-packed fast-moving mass of would-be settlers in search of territory to claim and hold. Thousands came by wagon; others trusted their futures to racing sulkies or high-wheeled bicycles. Hundreds leapt from specially chartered slow-moving Santa Fe trains. Still more simply ran through the buffalo grass and the prairie dog towns, looking for unclaimed land.

Even by Great Plains standards, Oklahoma has always been a stubborn and contrary place. Well after the territories all around were christened into statehood, it remained a blank space on the map. In atlases of 1880 an Oklahoma-sized void lay between established Texas and thriving Kansas, its panhandle reaching out to the intermountain West and desert Southwest beyond. Eighteen eighty-eight, and Oklahoma was still the last territorial holdout in the Southern Plains, though Dakota Territory, far above it, reached as far east. Eighteen eighty-nine, and the rivalrous Dakotas had achieved statehood, the order of their entry to the Union determined by a prudent and secret coin-flip. But Oklahoma was still a territory.

In 1907 it became a state. It was almost a Native American state. In 1905–7 Indian leaders, alarmed at pressures to open their remaining lands to homesteaders, lobbied to make much of what is now eastern Oklahoma the State of Sequoyah. It would have been populated by members of the Five Civilized Tribes (Cherokee, Choctaw, Seminole, Creek, and Chickasaw). None of these Native American nations was native to Oklahoma. All had been relocated from ancestral lands in Georgia, Florida, and Tennessee between 1819 and 1839—the journey known as the Trail of Tears—with a federal promise that the substituted Oklahoma territories would be theirs, in the sonorous and imprecise language of the treaty, "as long as the grass grows and the waters run."

Because the Republican majority in Congress feared, among other things, that the prospective Sequoyans would vote Democratic, the Sequoyah plan, to no one's surprise, met defeat. The Dawes Allotment Act had already opened lands in Indian Territory to white settlers; on April 22, 1889, more than twenty thousand had awaited the cannon blast that signaled the claim-staking rush. Like Guthrie and Norman, Oklahoma City was founded that day as a tent town, its streets and lots set out with chains and twine in the shortgrass meadows before the sun went down.

The Rush as pellmell coda to the westward migration remains the definitive Oklahoma moment. Restaurants serve Land Rush burgers; schoolchildren enact pageants about it still; a museum in Guthrie is dedicated to the 1889 event and to the lesser rushes that followed. The epic frenzy to claim and to hold remains a cache of emotional capital in a state where self-esteem runs chronically low. "We all went in together," white Oklahomans sometimes say still with relish. "All in one big bunch."

The Oklahoma Academy for State Goals is what the Land Rush wrought. Many of the crowd in the Sheraton's banquet room are the grandchildren of those who ran the fastest, in 1889 and after; the children of those who held the hardest. Now they are the leaders, the owners, the future-determiners, the claim-stakers, or could be.

"So much willed ignorance," says Sam Hurst to me, won-deringly, watching the last of the crowd descend the stairs. "They really don't want to hear."

Hurst is producing two NBC "Today Show" segments on the future of the Plains and on the Poppers' ideas. He has become a specialist on environmental stories, from livestock overgrazing in New Mexico (a project that netted him more than two thousand letters, mostly hostile) to examinations of the Colorado dam projects threatening sandhill crane migration along Ne-braska's Platte River.

A former campus political organizer, Hurst went halfway through a doctoral program in history before switching to other, swifter ways of teaching. Now he spends his life on planes. With his glasses and elbow-patched corduroy jacket, he could pass on campus as a rising scholar in the social sciences—fortyish, liked by the students, maybe a little vague on names—but though his face stays mild, almost sleepy, a head-jerk or finger signal brings instant response from his crew.

The "ABC World News Tonight" producer, Jayne Bruns, chain-smoking, petite, and morose, comes over to confer on logistics for the next day's expedition and is joined by Rutgers producer Linda Bassett. Bassett looks ruefully at Frank Popper as he dashes to confer, gray-suited arms windmilling, with Barry Serafin.

"Frank's driving us mad!" she says, *sotto voce*. "He wants to find a ghost town, *and* a buffalo mountain, *and* a shortgrass prairie. We'll need nine vans at this rate."

Only six, as it turns out. A twenty-person caravan of camera-men, producers, correspondents, and Poppers (plus the chair of the University of Oklahoma's geography department, who has volunteered as guide) assembles at seven-thirty the next morning under the Sheraton's portico, stowing trunks, arguing over schedules, conferring by walkie-talkie, and generally blocking traffic. Early-rising convention-goers stop and stare, then wave their friends over. Joggers and street cleaners detour to watch. The crowd of interested bystanders is soon spilling over the curb and onto the circular drive.

A doorman looks hard at Frank Popper and the camera crews, then asks me quietly, "Miss, you're sure you wouldn't like a cab, to get away from these folks?" I decline. It is a mild and sunny late-autumn day, and we are ready to depart the Sheraton in search of bison. Two police cars discreetly follow us to the edge of town.

As the parade of vans moves into the rolling uplands south-west of Oklahoma City, Frank Popper and Sam Hurst begin talking about when and how private-property rights can be abridged for a greater ecological good. This is the pre-interview, when a producer feels out a subject, discovers what topics he or she can talk well on, decides what questions will make the best footage.

The crucible of television can bring odd results, especially with academics, who are notoriously poor interview subjects, just sophisticated enough to be nervous about talking into a lens but loath to give up the lecturer's style for the intimate, underplayed voice that works on tape. And glamour is not the Poppers' strong suit—Frank looks like a friendly butcher, and Deborah's only cosmetics are soap and water. As we drive past wheat and peanut fields, heading for the Wichita Mountains buffalo preserve, Hurst is trying to decide how hard his morning will be.

"We're desperately attempting to describe to Plains people how much smaller their world is becoming," Frank tells him.

The built-in paradoxes of the contemporary West quickly turn his language compressed and allusive. "A fax-and-FedEx frontier may lie ahead, or perhaps one that features primarily wolves, Wal-Marts, and nuclear waste dumps, or some combination of both. The region is at a choice point."

Deborah has been doing the *New York Times* crossword, rapidly and in ink. Now she looks up.

"Remember, the Commons interests lots of groups, most of whom dislike each other," she tells Hurst. "The buffalo rancher hates the cattle rancher, who hates the oilman, whose blood boils at subsidized farmers, who scorn the Bay Area environmentalist, who loves the romance of buffalo but would never order a buffalo steak except in a very trendy restaurant."

Hurst is startled by her sangfroid. "You're deliberately *encouraging* vying value systems, then, despite the hatreds already there?"

"The West is a big place," Deborah replies. "We're all having to deal with a national deconstruction of our excesses. Wilderness areas in national parks are already graded by sanitation and supplies. The Commons is really one giant conservation easement. But not a uniform one. In some units of the Commons, pat-a-buffalo, definitely. Elsewhere . . . Frank, remember the Iowa doctor who wrote us?"

"The rite-of-passage guy!" Frank exclaims. "He wants to propose a new ritual of American manhood once the Commons gets going: the fourteen-year-old male's buffalo hunt, preferably using flint-tipped spears, early Lakota style. Of course, that means you lose a few adolescents every year, like Masai being eaten by lions."

Hurst considers possible sound bites. "Living lightly on the land, then; nature calls the shots; a shift in national land ethic?"

Frank nods. "Land no one wanted in the first place. Patty Limerick says there has never been a John Muir of grass. These lost sections of America badly need that. We, in our hubris, volunteered."

The caravan is passing through the dryland farms of Comanche County, with the weathered gray granite of the Wichita Mountains already visible ahead. November on the Northern and Central Plains is monochrome, but just past the 99th meridian southwestern Oklahoma is full of color still. Russet post oak and yellow cottonwood leaves flutter along the Washita River. Its waters run red, like the cinnamon earth in the fields it bisects, many touched now with the faint sea-green of young winter wheat. Here and there lie fallow stretches, where white-faced Herefords wander through dried cornstalks or ash-colored sheep walk slowly, breast-high, through tangles of dried weeds.

After a moment Frank says, "There is a downside to the Buffalo Commons. It could be a real disaster, a wasteland, unless managed at least as intensively as the national parks."

Deborah makes a face. "This generation of ranchers and farmers cannot be the ones to accept it," she points out. "They're already locked in to and rewarded by an agriculture based on heavy inputs of capital, fertilizer, pesticides, intensive grazing. But their kids, who go off to the land-grant schools and learn to think about sustainable agriculture and active management, will have to bring home a new sensibility. *If* the schools are savvy enough to adjust to these new demands and not cling blindly to the old agribusiness model. *If* the students and the schools love their region enough. It's like the military philosophy: 'Fight smart, stay alive.' "

Frank snorts. "Not to be Draconian, but there aren't *that* many ranchers. It might be better to pay 'em off and ship 'em back to Oklahoma City. Like every other Plains state, this is a subsidized, exporting economy. People, oil, farm products stream out, federal subsidies for petroleum, lead and zinc, welfare, agriculture, and defense pour in. It all used to work, but not anymore. Historically speaking, we're the next logical step."

Sam Hurst looks from one to the other. "Do you people often fight about the shape of the Commons?"

"Never," says Frank.

"All the time," says Deborah.

Her husband points out the window. Fifty yards away, in a field of blowing grasses, nine enormous buffalo have risen to their feet. They are ambling directly toward us, horns gleaming in the thin November sun. We hurry out of the vans to stand in the cold north wind and watch their deliberate, head-swinging progress. With immense dignity, and many hoarse sighs, the bison settle to the ground once more, this time at roadside, directly under a No Parking sign.

"I thought you said these buffalo were wild!" the Rutgers producer hisses at Neil Salisbury, the silver-haired geography professor who has led us here. Salisbury removes his pipe from his mouth and shrugs.

"They're imported buffalo," he points out. "And very video-savvy." He is right; as the crews unload and set up a half-million dollars' worth of television equipment, the buffalo exhibit polite interest but no alarm.

"Imported from where?" I ask.

Neil Salisbury grins. "New York."

The last sighting of a substantial wild buffalo herd within what is now Oklahoma occurred in 1876. In 1883, two Oklahoma Panhandle ranchers caught and raised a pair of buffalo calves, then decided to donate both animals to their old home-town, Keokuk, Iowa. Offspring of the Keokuk pair became mascots to the Page Woven Wire Fence Company of Adrian, Michigan ("A fence that will stop a buffalo will stop any farm animal"). In 1904 the New York Zoological Society bought four of the Page Company herd and shipped them to Manhattan.

In 1905 President Theodore Roosevelt (who in his twenties had hunted buffalo in the Dakotas) declared the Wichita Mountains' 59,000 acres a national game reserve. In 1907 he pressured Zoological Society officials to ship fifteen of its speci-men herd back to Oklahoma to restock the new refuge. By 1956 a thousand buffalo lived at the Wichita Mountains site, with others of the herd sent periodically to American and European zoos. In 1990 the herd numbered about 525.

The buffalo decide to rise and browse once more, and the humans follow. Frank and Deborah, each trailed by a parka-clad network crew, wade off in different directions through waist-high grasses, pausing on various rises to be posed, and posed again. It takes many minutes until Hurst and Bruns and the Rutgers team are satisfied with their shots of geographer and land-use planner near grazing beasts under a cirrus-touched aquamarine sky. Directly above the great brown backs of the buffalo a faint half-moon glows.

"Nice," says Jayne Bruns, with her first smile of the day. The ABC soundman checks his levels and nods. "Rolling," says the camera operator, and Barry Serafin begins to question Frank Popper, easing him along with intent stares and encouraging nods until Frank's voice drops an octave and passion for the topic wins out over taping terrors. Two knolls away, her bangs blowing wildly in the prairie wind, Deborah jams brown-gloved fists deep into her jacket pockets and smiles at Sam Hurst, who feeds her question after question as the camera rolls.

Along the narrow road that runs through the reserve, tourists with license plates from Pennsylvania, Saskatchewan, and New Mexico pull over to watch, looking first out into the buffalo pasture, then over at Neil Salisbury and me: *Should we know those people out there?*

We shrug. Out among the bending grasses the huddles of figures and equipment look very small. When I kneel to tie a sneaker lace, the shortgrass as seen from the eye-level of a reclining buffalo envelops me like a Dürer watercolor; streaks of amber, chestnut, rust, and rose-gray shine along the blue grama stalks and foxtail barley leaves, the lupine and bindweed. Below the wind-tangled crowns of the prairie grasses, in the cool, dim stalkage of the prairie floor, ebony beetles and plump golden spiders are investigating furrows of water left from last night's rain.

In academic life, to look like one's specialty is considered a good career augury. "Perfect for the period!" is a compliment, and not all that rare; medieval historians, with a change of clothes, could often pass as fourteenth-century monks. Renaissance-literature researchers tend to have Renaissance faces. Perhaps owing to their late entry into academe, perhaps to some insistent waywardness, the Poppers have not quite managed this melding of subject and self. If you met them at an American Association of University Professors convention, their disciplines would be hard to guess.

But Neil Salisbury, large and solid, is physiognomically correct in all respects for a physical geographer. After a life with landforms he has learned stillness, and can blend into landscape like a granite boulder. In a yellow Lands' End windbreaker, smoking his omnipresent pipe, a stiff north wind lifting his shaggy gray hair, he stands in the prairie grass and watches the filming progress without evident impatience. Salisbury is from Minneapolis.

He taught geography at the University of Iowa for twenty-four years and has been at the University of Oklahoma for twelve, specializing in fluvial geomorphology and natural resources.

At the moment he is telling me what a peculiar state Oklahoma is. Geology, ecosystems, accents, he claims, all defy easy mapping. Annual rains are under twenty inches in Oklahoma's western or Plains sections, as opposed to fifty-six inches at the other end of the state—that southeastern corner long called Little Dixie in honor of the resident alligators, cypress swamps, water moccasins, and Ku Klux Klanners. Neil drives the Plains in all weathers, conducting surveys of cultural and physical geography, or else crossing them on the way to some livelier geological region. He has seen the Plains in dry periods, and also remembers the boom years of the sixties and seventies, when Nebraska farmers were doing so well that Neiman Marcus regularly dispatched whole fashion shows to tiny towns in the Sand Hills, and the credit cards flew.

The TV crews thrash back toward the road. ABC wants to record the Poppers in a dying small Plains town (two towns, preferably). NBC has a filming appointment the next morning with a rancher near Rapid City, South Dakota. That's eight hundred miles away as the sandhill crane flies, but the presence of the bulky television equipment is forcing producer and crew to make a sixteen-hundred-mile detour via Chicago, owing to the lack of north-south jet service on the Plains.

"Out of sheer crass commercialism, don't tell ABC we're going to South Dakota," murmurs Sam Hurst as the van doors slam. Once back in the studios at Burbank he will supervise editing of the Popper and South Dakota material into two six-minute "Today Show" segments, then write the voiceover script for Bryant Gumbel. Jayne Bruns and Barry Serafin, in Washington, D.C., will craft their two days of footage into a four-minute "American Agenda" report for Peter Jennings's evening news. The country may see twenty or thirty seconds of Deborah and Frank at the banquet and on the prairie—pictures and sound— or a ten-second flash, or they may be edited out altogether. It is too early to tell.

After a brief stop at the wildlife preserve headquarters, where the rangers are calculating the fall elk hunt on their Samsung computers, Neil Salisbury leads the Poppers, me, and the Rutgers and ABC contingents deeper into western Oklahoma. We are heading toward Deborah's distressed counties and the prospective ghost town of Cooperton (pop. 31 and dropping). Salisbury is a field man, not a bench man, as they say in the sciences. His research hours are passed on Colorado rock glaciers or in the South Dakota Bad Lands. Our journey crosses lands less intimidating but just as devoid of settlement. Under Neil's guidance, in three hours' traverse of backroads Oklahoma, we encounter only twelve cars, four people in farmyards, dozens of wild turkeys, a threesome of trotting elk, and a tribe of Texas longhorns, dun and dappled and gray-black, their horns six feet from tip to tip. More turkeys. More elk.

"Look! Polar bears!" cries Frank, and everyone whips around, except Deborah, who is brooding on the issue of accuracy in media.

"These TV people point a microphone at me," she mutters, "and say, 'What do you think of when you see this country?' *I* don't know: Real purty? Lots of it? I'm not an actress. I have real conversations, not pretend ones. At least I used to."

In Cooperton the pretending starts in earnest. The Rutgers and ABC producers, drunk on visuals of civilization's decay, call for walking-feet-on-dusty-streets shots, through-the-blowing-leaves shots, rusted-windmill-against-the-sky shots. The Poppers are wired for sound and sent up and down crumbling cement sidewalks, into decrepit weathered sheds, onto the sagging porches of empty houses with caved-in roofs where gourd vines twist through broken windowframes.

Cameras and Poppers disappear completely into a thicket at one point, accompanied by much thumping and rustling. Neil Salisbury pushes aside branches to track their progress, then withdraws his head from the tangle of Osage orange, rolling his eyes.

"They're getting very creative now. Frank and Deborah are supposed to be staring wistfully through the windows of an abandoned house. You watch, someone will want a sunset shot next."

They do. It is still not enough. The cameras need pictures that tell a story, but the Plains just sit there, silently depopulating, and the remaining residents of Cooperton remain firmly indoors.

Wiser in the ways of Plains interviewing, Neil Salisbury finally lures a seventy-year-old retired schoolteacher into camera range by circling the dead mesquite tree in her backyard with a look of rapt admiration, till she is overcome by curiosity, and emerges. They discuss the beauties of her tree, the virtues of west Oklahoma mesquite (real purty, lots of it), the weather, the crops. Cold drinks and cookies are offered, and declined. Only then does Neil lead the talk, by courteous indirection, to the throng of impatient strangers who wait with cables and cameras ten feet away. The schoolteacher recognizes Barry Serafin and is not impressed; knows all about the Buffalo Commons, and does not approve.

"The only way you'll get me out of here is in a pine box," she tells Frank Popper, speaking firmly and well. "I was born in this house in 1920. I can go for a walk at four in the morning and not fear being robbed or killed. That total safety, that knowing the history of every stone and soul I see, is worth a lot. Can you Eastern people claim as much?" Frank tactfully studies the toes of his tennis shoes. The retired schoolteacher smiles, with more than a hint of triumph.

In low late-afternoon sunlight our caravan roars down the silent main street of Gotebo, Oklahoma (pop. 457), fifteen miles west of Cooperton. "Oh, God, perfect! Golden prairie light on a decaying small-town crossroads!" cries Jayne Bruns. Deborah tosses me her purse to hold as the network producer propels her toward the cameras, already waiting beside a ruined drugstore's crumbling mosaic archway.

By land-use planning standards Cooperton is a nearly dead town, but Gotebo is a generation behind it on the curve of decline. At its peak Gotebo was clearly quite a place. During Land Rush days it was a tent town, and it burned down once before permanent structures went up. Between 1900 and 1920, the four-block downtown rose and flourished, a collection of ornate two-story inventions in stucco, rosy brick, and soft gray stone. Carved Romanesque arches, proud keystones, acanthus-wreathed lintels, rusticated facades—all are boarded up now. In wrecked and crumbling foundations young trees grow. Though Gotebo's sidewalks are mostly gone to grass and weeds, every curb is scrupulously graded and posted for handicapped access with neat new blue-and-white signs. Discarded oil-well bits edge the yards of the occupied houses. From the four going concerns along the main street—swap shop, bar, garage, and city hall—elderly faces peer out under Stetson brims. "South Bronx goes Plains," says Deborah.

As the rich corn-colored light fades and cools, Gotebo comes alive. Phone lines have clearly been buzzing all over Kiowa County: between 4:40 and 4:43, nine pickups cruise by to check us over. One roars up and stops, releasing Reeder Reese, thirty-eight. He removes a red and white feed cap and scans us with care, his gaze lingering briefly on the Rutgers TV crew—one black, one female, one urban Italian. Exhilarated by a successful filming of the Great Plains sunset, they are now daring each other to enter Gotebo's bar and return in one piece.

"Y'all just leave Cooperton? My cousin there wants to write the Rutgers gentleman a letter."

Reese *is* Gotebo, it turns out: its truck-stop owner, fire chief, school board leader, building rehabber, and (young though he is for the job) its unofficial rememberer. His historical double vision of Gotebo past and present is extensive, and acute.

"There used to be Mason meetings in that hotel," he says, pointing to a roofless shell. "We used to have the variety store going, and the restaurant, and the American Legion hall. Bank and post office, too." With each lost activity and business named he points to a sagging or boarded-up structure along the street.

"We had a newspaper, with real hand-set type, until 'eighty-six or 'eighty-seven, when the editor died. The widow kept it going for a while, then she gave the equipment to the Smithsonian."

What local employment there is, Reese tells us, is limited to bar, rock crusher, and grain elevator. Several businesses have moved from central Gotebo to out near the highway, hoping to attract more out-of-town trade. "If we depended on the farms for business, we'd be dead already," Reese says. The Gotebo school district covers 597 square miles, with five hundred children

(K–12) bused in. But a consolidated school system is about to be put into effect.

"Cable saves us," Reese adds. "Everyone has HBO, ESPN, Cinemax. But my two sons won't stay in Gotebo, I know. They'll end up in Lawton, or Oklahoma City."

The briefest of shadows crosses his face. "I got married at twenty. Lost the chance for college. I had to stay, in a place where I know everyone I see, and always will."

The light is going in earnest now, turning rose and apricot and apple-green. A final scarlet flash is caught and repeated in the pothole pools all down the darkening street.

Our caravan splits up. The television people, as always, are on deadline, and need the next plane out from Oklahoma City, if they can find their way back across the prairies. "Put your glasses on, Barry, so you can read the map," his producer commands, and Serafin obeys. But Frank, Deborah, Neil Salisbury, and I are heading deeper into Buffalo Commons country. We wave good-bye to the ABC and Rutgers vans, and to Reeder Reese, and then swing west out of Gotebo, passing picked-over cotton fields and distant columns of oil rigs strung with lights. Behind me, in the darkened back seat of Neil's van, I hear Deborah grumbling.

"Couldn't I have read them just one footnote? A little one? Not an ounce of documentation all day is a terrible thing."

Frank sprawls, arms outflung, head draped over the seatback.

"I *love* television. All my life I've been impersonating academic dullness, never suspecting this other side of my personality. Now I discover that inside Modest Popper—'Go away, I want only to write'—is also Magisterial Popper—'The prairie, my friends, is a magnificent biosphere!'—and even Monomaniacal Popper—'I *am* the Great Plains!'"

Deborah: "Dear, may I make a suggestion?"
Frank: "Shut up?"
Deborah: "Riiiight."
Silence.
Then Frank: "But I'm so good at being superficial."
Neil Salisbury and I sneak a simultaneous glance at the back seat, just as Deborah puts her hand gently over Frank's mouth, and he kisses it. They lean against each other, holding hands, not talking. We drive on in the starlit prairie dark.

It is seventy-one degrees, a sunny November morning in Elk City, Oklahoma (pop. 9,579), and the Poppers are practicing cultural geography. Frank is hanging around the pool hall, drinking elderly coffee and watching elderly men in overalls play dominos. Over at Donnetta's Dress Shop, Deborah is trying on a hot-pink sequined dress with spaghetti straps and an explosion of silk roses near the hip—an artful lead-in to gender-specific interviewing of Beckham County residents on self-perceptions of sociopolitical elements integral to local economic stability. By the time she adds a matching sequined bandeau, then a forty-dollar belt of clear plastic studded with glass rubies, Deborah has unearthed some useful informants vying to describe Elk City's intricate round of Masonic dinners, Lions Club mixers, charity fashion shows, and church suppers.

I wander Main Street, eyeing the luxury trade: here a store selling postmodern country-and-western band gear (fringed Day-Glo T-shirts, Lucite drum sets, a neon sculpture of a buffalo skull), there a shop crammed with waterbeds, red-and-black flowered silk ties, and Brazilian herbal teas. Oil-money goods. Neil Salisbury stays in the van, studying a pile of the elegantly detailed maps issued by the American Association of Petroleum Geology in Tulsa.

"You can't do physical geography and cultural research at the same time; it's very confusing, like patting your head and rubbing your stomach," he explains austerely.

We flatten his maps against the steering wheel, and I see a burst of color all around Elk City: the magenta that signifies gas fields, chrome yellow for gypsum, black for silica sand, white for rock salt, and underlying all, the intense Ticonderoga blue of oil.

Elk City is in Beckham County, midway down Oklahoma's western edge. It is another McCook, surviving and even thriving, and Deborah needs to know why. She moves from dress shop to shoe store to bank to cafe to gas station, talking to locals, assessing the social web. According to her computers, Beckham is a rarity on the Plains, one of only 36 stable counties in the 435-county region where population has been steady for decades, neither declining nor booming, from census to census.

In Elk City's case this stability is due largely to the rich minerals lode of the Elk City Pool, discovered in 1947. We are in the heart of drilling country, not as thriving as it was in the boom years of the eighties but still holding its own. The Beckham County horizons are pierced by the columnar rigs of valves and piping that pump crude oil from rock laid down 60 million years ago. Gas-oil separators extract the natural gas and send it north and east by pipeline. The oil goes to refineries in Oklahoma, Texas, or Louisiana for conversion into gasoline, diesel fuel, kerosene, petrochemicals.

Outside Elk City two roads diverge, to our collective regret. A good deal of history lodges in the quiet acres hereabouts. Thirty miles north is the faint track of the California Road, first traveled by gold seekers in the spring of 1849 under cavalry escort. Near that is the willow grove on the Washita River where in the winter of 1868 George Custer's troops fell on the unprepared encampment of Chief Black Kettle, killing some two hundred men, women, and children, a gesture that left Custer a marked man among the Cheyenne and their sometime allies the Sioux. State Highway 34, running north and east near Elk City, roughly follows the route of the Chisholm cattle trail. An estimated ten million longhorns walked the Chisholm trail to Kansas railheads during the twenty-five years following the Civil War. The nearby Western Trail was established after the rise of barbed-wire fencing (and the custom, hastily instituted by the Chickasaw, of charging ten cents a head for every herd that crossed their land) made the Chisholm unprofitable.

Rather than tracing the migrations of cattle or Custer, we drive southwest on Route 66, the way of the Dust Bowl migrants, the Joad road. The tawny, undulant fields on either side are dotted with small stripper wells, their walking beams bending and rising like slow prehistoric scavengers. A few stand immobile. The little wells often idle part of the day, to let oil seep back into the bore. Some may draw only ten barrels in twenty-four hours, but though there are quicker ways to persuade crude from the ground—acid washes, nitroglycerin blasts, steam injection—their operators are patient about oil's eccentricities. At the height of the last energy boom nearly 100,000 oil wells, major and modest, were at work in Oklahoma. Now, about 70,000 are. Before the sabotaging of the Kuwaiti fields the entire Middle East operated only about 2,000 highly prolific wells. But Saudi and Kuwaiti and Iraqi petroleum rises almost too easily, in oil springs and seepages, pitch pools and asphalt lakes. Oklahoma is deep-well country.

"Fifteen miles northwest of Elk City, near Sweetwater, is the deepest rig in the world," says Neil Salisbury. "Exxon-owned."

Route 66 runs us deep into the mild dun rangeland of western Oklahoma. We are not yet to the dry heart of the Great Plains, which is known as the High Plains, and will not be for a hundred miles, but already the air feels drier, and sagebrush and soapweed appear along the fencerows. The altitude is climbing, the rainfall shrinking.

The Texas-Oklahoma border country we now traverse shares a century-old name with the Oklahoma Panhandle above it: No Man's Land. The shortgrass ranches and dryland farms are punctuated by low rocky buttes, and all the vistas are treeless, except for tangled gray-green clusters of mesquite and the rare imported windbreaks of poplar and Russian olive. In the 1880s an attempt was made to forest the Plains by encouraging home-steaders to create tree claims, areas set aside for fast-growing softwoods. Arbor Day was invented by Nebraska and Kansas in the 1870s. Agronomists believed that a treed Plains would un-dergo climate change and become more amenable to farming, just as they believed that rain follows the plow. Most of the original tree claims died in the droughts of the 1890s. In the Dust Bowl years, Plains residents were again encouraged to plant windbreaks as a stay against erosion; many did, but that crop of trees is reaching the end of its lifespan now. Many were cut down in the 1970s and 1980s to permit fencepost-to-fencepost farming. Replacement plantings are infrequent.

Until 1901 three million acres of the territory we are crossing belonged to the Kiowa and Comanche. The tribes announced a land rush that year and sat back expectantly. Nobody came. The land was too dry, too flat, too far from the railroad for anyone to want it.

"A Buffalo Commons makes perfect sense here," says Frank Popper, peering at a turkey vulture sunning itself on the hot asphalt and considering our potential as roadkill. "Country this empty is designed for them, not for us."

Land-use arguments are nothing new to these prairies. "Picking up bones to keep from starving," its reluctant settlers used to sing:

> Picking up chips to keep from freezing,
> Picking up courage to keep from leaving,
> Way out west in No-Man's-Land.

This has always been second-choice ground. The Comanche moved across it in territorial skirmishing but saved their real energies for the richer acres near present-day Kansas. Since 1629 it has been included in land claims by fourteen different governments, royal, territorial, and state; Texas, Kansas, New Mexico, and Oklahoma have all argued its ownership, not very strenuously.

Oklahoma won, and a generation later saw most of its acquisition blow away in the Dust Bowl. By the late 1930s 150,000 square miles of southwest Kansas, southeast Colorado, northeast New Mexico, and the Oklahoma and Texas Panhandles—nearly a third of the Plains—looked very much like desert. By 1940 the six inches of shortgrass topsoil that could sustain—barely—a West Oklahoma dryland farm had vanished, heading toward the Atlantic and the Gulf of Mexico in the form of wind and water erosion. Dust Bowl dirt clouds were five miles high and large enough to hinder airplane traffic on the Eastern Seaboard and to obstruct navigation by ships three hundred miles out on the Atlantic. By the start of World War II a hundred thousand Model T–loads of refugees had fled west along Route 66. The Plains-wide drought of the 1950s struck this country again; as did the 1963–67 drought; as did the 1975–78 drought; as have the dry eighties and the even dryer nineties.

We are passing through Mayfield, Oklahoma (pop. 17), one block long, eight miles from the Texas border.

"But in country as barren as this, how do you *know* when a drought is going on?" I ask, remembering the angry rancher from eastern Oklahoma at the Academy dinner, a linen napkin with buffalo-gravy stains twisted hard between his hands, shouting at Frank and Deborah that Plains dryness is only a passing phase.

"That's how," says Neil Salisbury, pointing through the windshield at a solar-powered rain gauge of battered tin, three feet tall, lashed to a plywood stand in a vacant lot. We swerve off the two-lane asphalt and brake beside an abandoned cellar hole. In Mayfield, Oklahoma, parking is free and plentiful. Mayfield consists of a filling station, a propane tank, seven modest houses of clapboard and corrugated metal, a hungry-looking red-tailed hawk atop a telephone pole, and a one-room general store that doubles as the post office.

"They may not talk to us," Neil Salisbury warns as we approach the battered screen door. "Or they may call the state patrol. Not many strangers show up around here."

In the store's dim, cool interior, 30 percent of Mayfield's residents—five very old men—sit over a noon meal of chocolate milk and barbecue potato chips. Four hunch in vinyl-seated kitchen chairs, which have been set in a semicircle on the concrete floor; the fifth has claimed a grimy plaid recliner near the soda-pop machine. Their midday entertainment is the wall-mounted police scanner, which crackles periodically: a speeder

caught near Delhi (pop. 23); a suspicious-person report in Tex-
ola (pop. 106). After each transmission, one or another of the
lunchers comments, but without any hurry. To a northern ear,
Mayfield vowels are slow and burbling, the lag time between
sentences unnervingly long.

"Signal's breaking up today," observes the overalled retiree in
the recliner, contemplating his bag of chips. "Storm coming. Or
something."

The others ignore him, preferring to supervise a sixth geriatric
compatriot who shuffles the aisles in search of Dristan and
yams. We wait. Mrs. Thomas Logan, the proprietress, wraps
these purchases tidily in paper and string, a service I have not
seen performed in years. Then she looks us over. That we are
professors and interested in the rain gauge outside reassures her
not at all.

"May I ask why you're asking all these questions?" she inquires. But soon she is telling us the names and ages of everyone
in Mayfield—no resident under sixty—and then she consents to
retrieve her husband from out back.

Since 1949 Mr. Thomas Logan has kept Mayfield's rain rec-
ords, inscribing them every week on the tissue-paper pages of
his official U.S. Government ledger. In all, forty-one years of
gauging.

"And no vacations," he says. "I wouldn't trust anyone else to
take the readings right. Or to mail the results in on time to
Washington." On the wall of the store, above the tapioca and the
canned peaches, hangs a framed certificate with a gold seal, an
award from the Meteorological Service for meritorious volunteer
service. I am glad to see it.

Mr. Logan turns the yellowing ledger pages slowly, so we can
admire the columns of numbers. His earliest entries were writ-

ten with a fountain pen; his newest are inscribed in felt-tip marker. At 1956 his finger pauses: 1.6 inches of rain from one January to the next. "That was bad," he says. "A bad year."

"All years are bad," says one of his ancient customers, without looking up.

"That's a pretty encouraging use of my tax money," comments Deborah as we cross the road once more.

"The highest-quality, lowest-cost scientific data ever produced," Neil Salisbury replies. "In every little settlement across the Plains since World War II there has been a rain watcher. It's the only secure climatological record American science possesses. They have been extraordinarily conscientious."

"Have been?" I say.

He rolls his eyes. "The U.S. Weather Service is cutting the program. They feel it's too low-tech."

To cheer ourselves we stop in Shamrock, Texas (pop. 2,259), for a rib-sticking lunch at the U Drop Inn Cafe: vegetable-beef soup, chicken-fried steak, real mashed potatoes with brown gravy, fried okra, pinto beans, black-eyed peas, and raisin pie. Neil, at sixty-two, is nonetheless the fourth-youngest customer and owns the youngest set of wheels. The couple in the next booth, we notice, arrived in a '51 Chevy. On the way out the door Frank buys two snazzy black feed caps bearing the Route 66 logo, one to wear, one to take home for Nicholas.

Collingsworth County, in the Texas Panhandle. Forty miles across, pop. 2,600. We have left the last oil fields on the other side of U.S. 40 and are headed straight south into Texas on narrow county roads, through level land and changing light. The skies are clear still, but the horizon has become so huge that you have to turn your head from shoulder to shoulder to scan it all. The land we traverse has been grassland for a million years, maybe two million. Now it is cattle-grazing country, sort of; what most of the shortgrass Plains would look like without extensive irrigation, what much more of the Plains will return to, if the Poppers are right.

"Buffalo would only improve this landscape," says Deborah, shuffling computer printouts.

"Pretty desolate," I say.

"Very desolate," says Frank.

"*Extremely* desolate," amends Neil Salisbury. He points out the red soil in the road cuts. "Shales and clay. The paler sections are sandstone and evaporates, like gypsum and salt. It means we're in the Permian Basin, where hardly anything grows. No real fossil or pollen record here. Very enigmatic country."

At twenty after three we cross the Red River, its sandy banks softened by a thick gray-green scrub of tamarisk and salt cedar. "River" seems a courtesy title for this wide clay flat with a thin ribbon of alkaline water down the middle. In some places the shallow flow is ten or twelve feet broad. In others it could be straddled by a preschooler.

"What is this, a temporary river?" says Deborah. No one replies. Neil tries the radio, but we are so far from anywhere that he can pick up only a blurred and static-ridden snatch of country and western, and then nothing. We drive on in silence, listening to the hum of tires on asphalt. North Texas is like an early Warhol movie, seventeen hours of watching a stranger sleep. The road swings up the wide Red River Valley of the song and the movie. From this valley they say you are going. Not fast enough.

"This is terrible country!" Deborah bursts out violently, almost gasping for breath. She is as close to losing it as I have ever seen her, pale as the gray-white undersides of the cottonwood leaves in the distant river bottom. Roaring crowds, furious farmers, armed platform bodyguards, packs of network television cameras, all are nothing to this sudden wave of despair brought on by an eight-hour crossing of western Oklahoma and the Texas Panhandle. She is like someone wading into a lake, going deeper, doing fine, who then walks off a hidden ledge beneath the surface and begins to drown. "There is *nothing here*. This is un-country. It shouldn't be allowed to exist."

We peer out the windows of the van. She has a point.

"Just like *Giants in the Earth*," says Frank dismally. "Expose the wife to the Great Plains, and she goes crazy."

"Don't *you* feel it?" Deborah asks me, half angry, half pleading, but I can only shake my head. This is the least appealing stretch of the Plains I have ever seen, but I still find the miles of nothingness soothing—some ancestral legacy held dormant in the crowded East, perhaps, or a half-memory of childhood journeys to Pierre, reading Laura Ingalls Wilder books in the back of the station wagon for six hundred miles.

But even inside Neil's tidy van, airline tickets securely pocketed, cookie supply ample, we are learning the strain of flatland. Every early settler on or visitor to the Great Plains, male or female, seems to have found the ceaseless winds, the heat, the deadening cold, the lack of human company in some degree hard to bear (except for emigrants from the Russian steppes, who felt quite at home and frequently said so). But space and silence, especially in the drabber stretches of the Plains, could also produce disorientation, depression, terror, madness. Where some newcomers felt profoundly liberated by the open places, others could be overwhelmed, prostrated even, by the same landscape. The sensation could last an hour, a day, or a lifetime.

It was like altitude sickness, or seasickness; there was no way to tell, in advance, how you would react. "Without trees or hills as cues to scale, there's no grounding, no place to hold on to," says Deborah, eyes tightly closed.

The Plains are most interesting when studied in an unfolding sequence, commons style. You graze, and you move on. The allure is in the passing through. It is country built for motion, country where motion equals hope. ("They've got the dwindles," people whisper on the Plains, if a friend or relation takes to sitting and staring for no good reason. In a region whose unofficial motto is "Keep Moving or Die," it is not a diagnosis lightly pronounced.) The early settlers, between chores, did a lot of sitting and staring.

In the 1940s a Nebraska social historian named Everett Dick collected hundreds of accounts of prairie life that chronicle how deeply the physical geography of the Plains—Northern, Central, and Southern—affected the women who came there. Homesteader's wives raised in the green East with carpets underfoot and gaslight overhead, clean sheets on the bed and hothouse lettuce on the table, often adjusted with extreme difficulty, or not at all.

"There was nothing to see and nothing to do," Dick notes, summarizing the testimony of early journals, letters, and memoirs. "The conversation each day was a repetition of that the day before, and always concerned the terrible place where they had to live. Even the children felt the monotony of the life. One day in the eighties a little boy came into the sod house to his mother and, throwing himself on the floor in hopeless grief, exclaimed, 'Mamma, will we always have to live here?' When she hopelessly replied in the affirmative, he cried out in desperation, 'And will we have to die here, too?' "

Well, yes. The cowboy dirge "O Bury Me Not on the Lone Prairie" reflects accurately the last wishes of many. New Englanders were notorious in early Plains society for frantic deathbed pleas to have their bodies shipped back East, wanting only to be buried as they had not lived, near water and trees.

Hall County, Texas (pop. 5,594). For the last forty miles Neil's tour notes on this limbo of pale sky and leached earth have turned sparse. ("Horned toad." "Barbed-wire fence." "Feed mill." "Sagebrush." "More sagebrush." "*Burned* sagebrush.") Now he simply points, and we nod. Soon there are no more feed mills. Then, no more fence.

" 'In the United States there is more space where nobody is than where anybody is. That is what makes America what it is,' " Frank Popper and Neil Salisbury chant, in imperfect unison.

"Gertrude Stein. *The Geographical History of North America*," adds Deborah. At last, a footnote. She is appeased, herself again, and just in time. We are approaching the edge of the Llano Estacado—the Staked Plains—a stretch of Texas prairie so famously devoid of landmarks that early travelers and traders pounded stakes into the ground as they rode, to avoid death from undifferentiated geography.

Or buffalo stampedes. In 1878, O. W. Williams, a pioneer surveyor and frontier lawyer, was heading a surveying party in Lamb County, two counties west and one south from Hall County, where we are now. Up to that time, Williams later wrote, "the map of that county in the General Land Office was only a blank sheet." Though accustomed to the landscape of the Southern Plains, Williams was not pleased with his assignment to the Llano Estacado.

"I believe that I have never looked upon any other country so destitute of the graces which go to make up what we call scenery as this plain," he wrote in his journals,

> . . . it might have been a dead world. There was no movement; even the birds of the air were not to be seen. Nor was there sound. But we could not consider it a desert, so long as that spring kept up its flow and that grass sward lay so solidly on the dark red earth.
>
> We ran our line of meander down a creek, two chainmen and two flagmen afoot, while I carried the transit from station to station on horseback. As I was setting up my instrument, my flagman asked if I heard a peculiar sound. I stopped my work to listen and caught, from the north, a faint throbbing of somewhat irregular cadence such as I had heard two years before, when twenty miles from Niagara Falls. What seemed to be a low-lying cloud was sweeping down on us. We were for a moment at a loss to account for it. Since it was late July, it could hardly be a norther. Almost at once the cry went up: "Buffaloes! A stampede!"
>
> We stood in single file, facing the oncoming herd. With the only rifle in the party, naturally I was at the head of the file, in order to split the passing animals with the firing of the gun. We were barely ready when they were on us with a swirl of dust and a thunder of hooves—yet so far as I could judge, they were absolutely mute. The front line was thickly packed, shoulder to shoulder. I began firing, because it began to look as if they might run over us without seeing us. I commenced to shoot as rapidly as possible but without effect until they were thirty feet away. At that point I saw some of the animals in front of me begin to push their neighbors to one side or the other to make an opening, about twelve feet wide where the front line passed us, although it seemed to me that I could touch a buffalo on either side with the point of my gun.

Beyond this dense line there was no regular formation; the animals came on in loose order, gradually thinning out to the rear. During the terrific uproar of the passing multitude, I had dimly made out sounds which might have come from the men or the horse behind me . . . but when I turned I found a horse that was trembling, and four men exceedingly dust laden and full of strange oaths, but nothing to show that we had been in danger. . . . The rest of our party [which had seen the event from greater safety] estimated the number in the stampede at fifty thousand.

The herd was almost surely the last great herd of the Southern buffaloes after they had been cut off from any migrations to the north, and after five years of the Sharps rifle in the hands of the professional hunters.

Remembering Williams's account, I turn around in the front seat of the van to look at Frank and Deborah.

"Will there be buffalo stampedes on a Buffalo Commons?" I inquire. "Stands to reason," says Frank.

Quitaque, Briscoe County, Texas. A one-street, ten-block town. Population unknown. Since crossing the 98th meridian on the way out of Oklahoma City, we have been traveling the Great Plains, but only now have we reached the official edge of the region's dry heart, the High Plains. These are signaled by the tabletop plateau called the Caprock Escarpment, which rises like a great winding wall just outside Quitaque, its cliffs of cream-colored calcium carbonate, or caliche ("ca-*lee*-chee"), riding atop the brick-red gravel of the Ogallala aquifer.

Caprock covers much of the High Plains, and the Ogallala owes its recharge to the caprock. The aquifer is not an underground sea, as the name suggests, but rather a subterranean layer of saturated stone (five-sixths gravel, one-sixth water) built by millennia of raindrops absorbed into Plains grassland. The recharging process is still going on at a stately pace, a portion of every meager rainfall percolating down, centimeter by centimeter, through sandy topsoil and thirty feet of caprock. But caliche is lime hardened to the consistency of cement, strong enough to resist anything but a charge of dynamite. Water can get through caliche, but it takes a while. In Texas, Oklahoma, Kansas, and Nebraska, a billion water-feet are lifted yearly from the ancient aquifer for irrigated farming. In 1950 central Kansas had 250 wells sunk into the aquifer; in 1990 it had over 3,000. In 1950 the Kansas portion of the aquifer was fifty-eight feet thick; today, in some places, less than six feet of moisture remain. The Great Plains would have to enjoy the rainfall of a Brazilian jungle for the Ogallala to keep pace with so relentless a draw.

The strain is showing. Near Floydada, Texas, one county southwest of Quitaque, the water table has fallen nearly one hundred feet in one hundred years. Cracks and sinkholes have begun appearing in the earth from Texas to Nebraska as the traumatized Ogallala settles, and settles again. Beyond the Ogallala's reach, drought and the politics of water are no less worrying. Periodic water rationing has been declared in towns and cities across South Dakota since 1989; South and North Dakota and Montana are currently suing the U.S. Army Corps of Engineers for increased access to the waters of the Missouri. To which the Corps replies: Get real. Every water-foot is spoken for, and then some.

Like the residents—the former residents—of other sections of the Plains, Quitaque's citizens appear to be voting with their feet. On a warm, clear Saturday afternoon, the silence in the central business district is absolute; no bird cries, no voices, no engines. Nothing. We wander the sidewalks and talk in whispers, like tourists at an archaeological site.

We do not know Quitaque's population, official or actual. Deborah has only the 1980 census figure (696 people); her 1984 Hammond atlas, beloved by geographers for its completeness, shows Quitaque on the map, but the town in which we stand has disappeared from the Texas index. Unlike in Gotebo there is no one to ask or even to talk to. On the door of the town's one semifunctioning hardware store hangs a sign, Call If You Want Anything, followed by a home phone number. The other stores along Quitaque's main street are not in ruins, like their Goteboan counterparts, but neither are they in business. Instead, each front window in each locked and defunct shop houses a still life, neatly arranged and labeled, of artifacts from Great Plains life circa 1870–circa 1960, when Quitaque still thrived. Visit Our Sidewalk Museum, says a sign painted on the side of the downtown's last building.

"It's a return of the false front," says Deborah wonderingly, peering at a careful arrangement of tin washboards and pie plates, a tangle of mule harness, 1920s wedding albums, and 1940s copies of *Life*. Quitaque, she concludes, is a town with a serious case of the dwindles.

When the Poppers look for other places in America where the indices of distress parallel those Deborah has compiled for the Plains, the closest matches lie in urban areas. To the eye of the geographer and the land-use planner, the growing decay in the heart of some American cities is not that different from the growing silence beyond the 98th meridian. Inner-city Oakland and Philadelphia are remarkably close cousins of Hayes Center and Gotebo. Lack of new investment and loss of population spell, for all, continued decline. Among politicians and planners, such connections are rarely made or, if understood, admitted—what is Newark to us, or we to Newark? But to the research scholar and the resident, the kinship of despair is perfectly clear.

"It's death by neglect, either way," says Frank Popper, pulling down the brim of his new feed cap. It makes him look almost like a native, especially when he remembers to add the slowed-down, toes-in walk favored on the Plains. That too may end up a lost social artifact, like flint arrowheads or the minuet, but he has always been interested in lost causes and last stands.

"There's less chance of being killed in a mugging or drive-by shooting out here, but in the long run that's about the only difference. It's like watching a very long, very painful train wreck. We're already into the aftermath. Kansas alone has over two thousand ghost towns. Frontier conditions are returning to the West, like it or not, but there are many kinds of frontier, most of them deeply uncomfortable and scary to live on, whether in Detroit, Michigan, or Quitaque, Texas."

The long road back to Oklahoma City takes us over the caprock, through the miniature badlands of Palo Duro State Park, and across the High Plains. The hardscrabble bleakness of the Oklahoma-Texas border country was emptiness without grandeur. But the High Plains are flatness perfect and absolute, level as a cup of flour swept with a knife.

" 'There was nothing but land,' " quotes Frank softly, from the beginning of Willa Cather's *My Ántonia*, looking all around him in wonder, " 'not a country at all, but the material out of which countries are made.' "

On the west rim of the world are the city lights of Amarillo, fifty miles off. In air this dry and still they do not twinkle but burn, distinct and steady, till the road takes us over the curve of the earth, and they are quenched, and nothing replaces them. As the land fades, only the sky tells us we are traveling.

Night does not fall on the Plains, it rises, and you can see it rising. We are moving straight north, acutely conscious of the Plains as a great swath of earth curving up over the globe from central Texas to the Manitoban forest and tundra. To our right, away from the setting sun, bands of clear color, each claiming a third of the cloudless sky, ascend toward the zenith: first cream, then above that the pale lavender of a wild geranium, then cobalt. To our left, the western half of the sky is daylight blue still, but a line of crimson and gold claims the horizon. As we watch, the cobalt color moves up the eastern sky and down the western, and the stars appear. The terminator, the ever-moving line between day and night, has passed over us and swept on toward the Pacific, leaving the land it has crossed in darkness.

Darkness, in New Jersey, is a relative term. There is no night there, not really—certainly not in New Brunswick, where thirty-five million people live within a hundred miles of Frank and Deborah's house, where half the sky is permanently stained with the hazy glow of New York and the other always bright with the light pollution of Philadelphia and the mid-Jersey sprawl. But in the heavens of the Southern Plains the stars are huge and strange, the Dipper and Orion lower down and more sharply tilted than on the rare nights we see them at home.

And these are the gentlest of the High Plains. Back on the eastbound interstate, to stay awake we talk of quintessential plains, but all the votes are different. Deborah wants to apotheosize eastern Montana, with its rolling rangeland, its sagebrush and medicine rocks, its county fairs with chokecherry jellies and canned grasshoppers for sale. Neil remembers western Kansas, where there is nothing but wheat and sky. I speak for South Dakota west of the Missouri in winter, with ground like iron and a sky like steel. Frank thinks of summer storms moving over central Nebraska, seen from a long way off, dragging dark tails of rain.

*　　*　　*

On Monday morning I explore the climate-controlled skyways and office-building atriums of Oklahoma City. Considerable stretches of the downtown seem to be reverting, Popper-fashion, into an unused terrain of tenantless retail space, empty halls, empty suites. There are 834,088 people somewhere in this state capital, but at high noon I go stand on the center line of Grand Avenue and am in absolutely no danger; there is not a moving vehicle in sight.

Oklahoma City is the kind of place that delights growth-minded people like Phil Burgess of Denver's Center for the New West. Oklahoma City is one of the great urban islands of the Southern Plains, a magnet of jobs and fresh starts for large stretches of Texas, Oklahoma, New Mexico, Colorado, and Kansas. But it still seems a city of convenience, not conviction. At a downtown newsstand with a small, hand-lettered sign, Hometown Papers, I watch men and women in suits and work shirts and fast-food franchise uniforms snatch up day- or week-old newspapers from smaller towns and cities all across the Southern Plains. The nameplates are a feast of Victorian optimism: the Larned *Tiller & Toiler*, Muskogee *Daily Phoenix & Times-Democrat*, Pecos *Enterprise*, Duncan *Banner*, Pueblo *Chieftain*, Lubbock *Avalanche-Journal*.

As no state lies entirely within the Plains, no major rail line links the Southern to the Central to the Northern Plains, and no interstate either, except the Billings–to–Santa Fe stretch along the front range of the Rockies and the San Antonio–to–Topeka highway on the eastern edge of the Plains. There is no city that acts as a cultural or political capital (as Atlanta serves the South). Nor are the Great Plains the base for any major newspaper which might provide a regional voice, as the *Boston Globe* does for New England. Newspapers on the Plains remain not far

removed, in spirit or in layout, from the single-sheet editions of
the sod house frontier, printed in the bed of a wagon on brown
butcher paper or wallpaper scraps, whichever was handiest.

I buy a dozen in the Oklahoma City newsstand display and sit
reading them on a nearby bench in the chill, still air, smiling in
recognition as I turn pages. They are all cousins to the Pierre
Capital-Journal, whose nepotistic mastheads have for sixty years
consisted of Hipples (president, George Hipple; production
manager, George Hipple; vice-president, John Hipple; business
manager, John Hipple; circulation, Brad Hipple; national adver-
tising, Terry Hipple).

There is an etiquette to reading a Plains paper, which I do not
violate. First the police blotter, to see if anyone you know has
been arrested. Then the social news: who went to lunch at
whose house, what they ate, what they wore. Next you read the
hospital reports, which are usually phrased with ominous dis-
cretion ("Mrs. Myrtle Weller of Okanago Township is doing as
well as can be expected"). Then, in stoic natural progression,
the obituaries ("Came to Coolidge from Mandan in 1911;
ranched there until 1959; retired to Laguna Beach but soon
returned"). Then the poet's corner, with its contributions from
readers:

> I found a rattlesnake in the kitchen
> I took the hoe, I hit him low
> I hit him, I hit him
> With much vim.

And finally the rainfall reports—always included, often set in
bold type—reported to the hundredth of an inch.

I want to see the 98th meridian again, so one of Oklahoma

City's few female cabdrivers and I travel the length of Reno Avenue, a four-lane artery stretching west out of town. Warehouses of stained concrete, rusting prefab sheds, and dying strip malls line the roadway. When we do cross the 98th meridian, the scenery suggests that we might as well be in Newark.

Raised on a ranch south of town, the driver tells me; worked the rodeo circuit from Idaho to Dallas; had a bad fall; came back here. No home to go back to; her folks sold the ranch when land prices were good and bought a little farm; farmed a year or two and went broke; sold the farm to a subdivision contractor and moved to Phoenix. She is thirty-five now and can make three hundred dollars on an eighteen-hour shift, easy, but only by working the late-night bar rush.

The cab's interior smells powerfully of Lysol, and she apologizes. "One of my steady customers got real drunk last night," she explains. "He started describing to me all the people he'd killed in Vietnam. Then he pulled out his glass eye to show me how it worked. Then he threw up. I got him home and up the stairs—he's a paraplegic—but I had to spend the entire morning at the car wash. I scrubbed the car out good, and dried everything with my blow dryer." I praise the results. She says it passes the time.

At the next strip mall I ask her to let me off; I want to look at Tenner's Western Outfitters, next to the Ninja Saloon and Dance Hall. But wedged between them is the Napoleon Cafe. Its fortyish proprietors (she blond and chic, he bearded and serious) keep color postcards of the Côte d'Azur tacked to the wall behind their cash register, right under the fading Frederic Remington reproduction. It is a wall they look at a lot.

"We are from Cap d'Antibes. We have been in Oklahoma six months. In New York, before this, five years," the husband explains, sliding an enameled serving dish of chicken chasseur into a display case already glowing with apricot slices bedded in puff pastry. Beside these are small mushroom quiches, crust edges deftly braided, and a battalion of tartes aux mocha. A Piaf tape sings in the five o'clock gloom. I am the only customer, and the owners understand my quick glance around the deserted tables.

"Why are you here?" I ask them hesitantly. They are self-contained people, proudly correct, but at my question they suddenly smile the same smile, an expression of radiant vision-ary joy that transforms both reticent faces. They had always wanted, they tell me, to go West. To see the prairies. To see the Indians. And to see buffalo? I ask. They look at me in sur-prise, a bit offended. "Certainly. Naturally. Buffalo most of all."

"Of course, it is as you see," the proprietor adds, with a small ironic handsweep that takes in the twilight highway, the con-crete warehouses, and the whooping Osage teenagers circling the parking lot in big-wheeled pickups, Bon Jovi tapes blasting. Along Reno Avenue oil tankers rumble past. Will they stay, I ask? Yes, they say, an overlapping chorus of affirmation. Yes, we will stay, yes, oh, yes.

In Oklahoma City in the 1920s thousands of oil derricks rose within the city limits, many within sight of downtown, a half dozen on the grounds of the state capitol building. Developers talked confidently of an oil well in every backyard until March 1930, when a well named the Mary Sudik ran wild, spouting ten thousand barrels each twenty-four hours. It rained oil for eleven days in Oklahoma City, the greasy brown-black spray reaching even the university town of Norman, fifteen miles south.

The Poppers are scheduled for a final talk in Norman, to undergraduates in the University of Oklahoma's honors program. No runaway oil wells or other excitements are in evidence, only another crowded room, another mass of television lights and cables, another largely hostile audience. Frank and Deborah are so tired that they have achieved a glassy-eyed calm, like political candidates who have been on the road for more hours than they can count or care to.

At the back of the lecture hall I encounter Bret Wallach, a geographer on the Oklahoma faculty, a MacArthur Fellow. Ascetic and dark-haired, arms crossed over a Scandinavian-patterned sweater, he is observing the Popper media circus with a skeptical eye.

Bret Wallach and Frank Popper had nearby offices at Resources for the Future in Washington, D.C., seven years back and have been arguing about the Plains ever since. Despite their jousting ("Frank publishes, I write"), Bret Wallach's readings of and reactions to landscape are often Frank Popper's second intellectual benchmark, Deborah's being his first. Articulate mavericks are hard to find, in the land arts.

"Geography is a field that deals with people," Bret Wallach tells me now, watching students climb over knees and backpacks to find seats for the Poppers' talk. "Too much social science baggage is poison for the imagination. Frank and Deborah are trying to awake imaginations. By guts and insouciance it may just work. They're not some nuts with a freaky idea—basically, the Commons resurrects the Land Utilization Program of the 1930s."

He gives me some of the history. Arthur Hyde, Hoover's

secretary of agriculture, was all in favor of what he called "a new epic" of land retirement. A few years later, urged on by the dreadful example of the Dust Bowl, the United States Forest Service announced that a minimum of 125 million acres appeared a conservative initial plan for the purchase of submarginal lands. Only 11 million were actually bought, most visible today as the present Forest Service–administered National Grasslands.

Wallach himself has proposed a grasslands-preservation strategy under which the Agriculture Department's Forest Service would enter into voluntary contracts with Plains farmers and ranchers, paying them the full value of what they would grow during each of the next fifteen years, but requiring them *not* to cultivate. Rather, they would replant to reestablish native shortgrass, after which time the Service, as part of the original contract, would buy out their holdings except for a forty-acre homestead, thus providing for the former owners, decreasing erosion, and expanding public lands in a system of Plains parks.

"But I agree with what Frank and Deborah want," Wallach says, watching Frank distribute handouts of Deborah's computer charts. "Ours are both strategies for regional deprivatization. The name 'Buffalo Commons' is a contribution in itself; it draws on deep instincts, just as the value of an intimate knowledge of the land is drawing away and vanishing from our national memory."

He looks toward the podium again, where Deborah is dealing with an agitated professor of range management, then turns back to me.

"The Plains are full of forbidden ideas," Bret Wallach says quietly. "As in 'Thou shalt not think about the bad years. Thou shalt not consider consequences. Thou shalt pretend the crisis is not there.' It's leading us to terrible trouble. I like the spaciousness of the Plains, the unboundedness of it. Which is fortunate. Because if Frank and Deborah have their way, we will go back not to 1880 or 1930, but to Francis Parkman."

When the Poppers get back to New Brunswick they have earned the enmity of the Rutgers mailroom yet again. A former Oklahoman, return address Chicago's Lake Shore Drive, wants to know if his childhood county is in trouble. (It is.) Opinions on the Commons have arrived from The Friends of Native Americans (return address Arlington, Massachusetts) and a South Dakotan now working as a screenwriter in Vermont: pro. Four farm wives in Kansas, con. The newly formed Buffalo Commons Chamber Music Society of Grand Forks, North Dakota, sends a concert notice (Mozart's Quintet in C Major, K. 515, admission free). A historical archaeologist in Trenton says that the Poppers' work has changed his life. A Nebraska folklore expert suggests that the Poppers are un-American publicity hounds and asserts that they (and everyone who listens to them) need immediate psychological help. A communications consultant in Manhattan wants to offer her design services for the Buffalo Commons newsletter ("What newsletter?" says Deborah). A number of people would like to know where to send their donations to the Buffalo Commons Foundation, to help preserve the prairies ("What foundation?" says Frank. "And will they consider a direct deposit to a numbered account in Zurich?"). A stockbroker in Minneapolis, an editor in Boston, an internist in Jacksonville, Florida, a college student in Kansas, a physician in Pueblo, Colorado, and an attorney in San Francisco all have identical queries: "What can I do to save the Plains?" The University of Wyoming library would like the Poppers to donate their research papers to the campus archives, which already contain the correspondence of Jack Benny and James Watt. A talk-radio host in Palm Beach wants to know if Frank will accept the post of Secretary of the Interior.

Three weeks later Sam Hurst's pair of "Today Show" segments air, showing Frank and Deborah besieged at the banquet table of the Oklahoma Academy for State Goals dinner, then footage from the buffalo reserve. CBS calls again, contritely; so does National Public Radio, and a British documentary filmmaker, and the *Dallas Morning News*.

The ABC footage of Frank and Deborah and Oklahoma proves handsomer yet. The flowing grass and the golden light look spectacular on tape; the Cooperton schoolteacher, erect and articulate; the land, very empty. All their relatives call them to say so, though Deborah's mother, watching in Florida, thinks her child deserved more airtime.

"Frank's hair looked just like waving wheat," Deborah tells everyone. Reactions on the Rutgers campus upon seeing scholarly colleagues wedged between the stock market news and the detergent ads range from mild pleasure through honest bafflement to arctic chill. A number of faculty members go out of their way to assure the Poppers that they never watch network television.

"Is this fun for you, Frank?" inquires a humanities dean, kindly, pausing beside the Poppers' table as he bears a cup of coffee through the second-floor faculty cafeteria near Lucy Stone Hall. Yes, yes it is, Frank Popper says. In the treeless pebblerock courtyard outside the winter afternoon is moving toward dusk, and snow has begun to whirl past the windows of the offices and computer labs. Only a scattering of students, down-vested, hurry along the sidewalks toward the dorms; in the dorms, only a few windows are lighted. New Jersey is so small a state that by noon on most Fridays Rutgers feels deserted. Its forty thousand undergraduates—nearly a tenth the population of Wyoming—swiftly out-migrate on the weekends, laundry bundles and chemistry problem sets in the car trunk, heading home on the Jersey Turnpike or the Garden State Parkway or along Route 1.

Sated with Commons mail–reading, I go into the Rutgers student union at dinnertime ("suppertime" on the Plains). Looking for a pay phone, I rove up and down the deserted halls. I have been here when the decibel level was excruciating—pounding music, yells of postadolescent high spirits or postadolescent complaint, the clash and clatter of food trays. Now only my footfalls echo down the marble corridors. Then I hear another set of footsteps, coming toward me around the next corner. A tall, skinny boy in a Nuke The Unborn Whales T-shirt wanders into view, swinging a backpack, peering at all the dark hallways, and the empty rooms. He seems thoroughly disgruntled. "What a ghost town," he says.

IV
WHERE THE
BUFFALO
ROAM

THE NORTHERN PLAINS:
Montana
and Wyoming

I T TAKES A LOT to make a Montanan scream, but a night landing in a March blizzard qualifies when the ground is a sheet of black ice and everyone on the plane knows what lies at the end of the runway at Billings International: the edge of a very high mesa. "Brakes, lady, the brakes!" growls the seventyish rancher beside me, wide hands gripping the armrest, buff Stetson sliding from his lap, but the pilot is already doing her best with the skewing, sliding plane.

We had been due in to Billings from Denver at five, and now it is nearly midnight. At the terminal's front door I watch the passengers from the rows around me disappear purposefully into the storm: the plump CPA in parka, strap sandals, and lei, returning to the nearby Crow Reservation from an accountants' convention on Maui; the Roundup High School wrestling team, sauntering toward their schoolbus with ski jackets left conspicuously unzipped even in the bitter night wind. I wince, and the sheep rancher standing beside me laughs. "I used to play frostbite chicken, too, when I was that age," he says. His wife pulls up in a four-wheel drive and leans across the front seat to receive two fat mesh bags of navel oranges, purchased in Orlando that morning. They live in Petroleum County (pop. 655), a hundred miles north, and can expect to make it home by daybreak if the weather turns no worse.

It is snowing so hard now that the flakes blow in horizontal sweeps off the edge of the rimrock and into the dark, the wind ululating and keening, headed for Moose Jaw. Eastern and central Montana sometimes identifies more with the prairie provinces of Canada than, say, Texas, and with reason; the Northern Plains of Montana sweep up to the border and keep going, transformed by a political but not a geographic line into the Southern Plains of Alberta, Saskatchewan, and Manitoba.

Even in a region of very large states, Montana is enormous, stretching the width of the Mountain time zone. One of ten Montanans lives in Billings (pop. 67,000), and most of them like to tell North Dakota jokes. Why can't you get ice cubes in North Dakota? The old lady who had the recipe died. What is the North Dakota state tree? The telephone pole. The jokes do not get any better.

I share a cab down off the airport mesa and into town with an attorney from Bismarck, North Dakota, who is not feeling humorous. She has come to watch a historic trial, potentially involving hundreds of millions of dollars, going on in Billings over Upper Missouri Basin versus Lower Missouri Basin water rights.

"The Indians are a real worry," she says, huddling into her red cloth coat till only eyes and nose show above the collar. Her voice is muffled and gloomy. "Tribal claims throw everything off. The Fort Peck Reservation won the right to enough water to cover a million acres one foot deep every year, which is a lot of water. The Wind River people got their tribal allotment, too. And a good twenty reservations are still out there just biding their time."

"There's ranchers screaming from here to Fargo on that one," says a bass voice from the front seat. The cab's heater broke yesterday at forty below, and the driver is a bundle of Gore-Tex and wool in the winter darkness.

Billings, which began life in the 1880s as a railroad siding, possesses a modest skyline of high-rise hotels and banks and a Yellow Pages full of alluring entries. Stores here sell petrified wood and dinosaur bones, caviar and cattleguards. There is a long list of suppliers for mining and oil-exploration explosives, and an equally long list of dealers in artificial limbs and eyes. I find listings for nannies and for neuropsychologists, fur skin brokers and pawnbrokers ("Guns, saddles, gold, large knives, bail bonds, computers accepted. Our motto: We Never Ask Why").

For early March, the National Weather Service reports the next morning are not bad: snow advisories east and west of the Continental Divide; snow in Kalispell; stockmen's and travelers' warnings for Cody and the western Dakotas. Monida Pass: fog. Six below zero in Cut Bank. Downtown Billings (9:00 A.M. windchill: twenty-six below) is a blur of dry lustrous powder. A ground blizzard is kicking up. Under pale, clear blue sky, cars drive with headlights on. It is so cold that the inside of my nose sticks together after three breaths, and the ice-cube air touching chin and cheekbones and the fingerspan between my brows freezes every centimeter of exposed skin first into pain, then to immobility.

Desperate for warmth I rush into a downtown mall, its pink and peach and neon hallways deserted except for a quartet of snowbound electricians from Laurel, fifteen miles west, hunting breakfast. They study a display of caramel rolls, chocolate-hazelnut coffee, and bottled Australian passionfruit juice. "Might as well," says one, breaking the ruminative silence. "You gotta eat."

A vanload of highschoolers rushes through the revolving doors, also looking for calories. A boy of fourteen, sturdy and very blond, stops dead beside me, too overwhelmed to be cool, staring at the glass elevator, the Benetton sweater displays, the slabs of crab quiche.

"Do you have a mall in your town?" I ask. "No," he admits, then adds, "but we're going to! Someday, I know it!" His chin goes out, and his eyes are fierce. It is a Plains look I know: the can-do, at-any-price, as-good-as-them, we'll-show-you expression, handed down like an heirloom west of the 98th.

Cautiously, hugging the yellow brick of the next few buildings, I advance through the whirling snow to a glossy interior-decorator's shop down the street. The proprietor, a Montana State University graduate in a striped Ralph Lauren shirt, tells me his clients are scattered across southern Montana and northern Wyoming. "Not the rich-rich, of course; we're not selling Louis Quinze here. Those people go to New York or San Francisco for what they want. We do homes for well-off farmers and ranchers."

I buy a fir-colored wool throw (from Maine), and the staff politely raise their brows at my New Jersey return address. I say I am in town to see the Poppers' talk.

"The buffalo people?"

I nod.

"Oh, my dear, not really!" They look around the showroom and laugh merrily. I can see why. The hand-loomed pillows, the topiary centerpieces, the faience and potpourri, the Brunschwig et Fils brocade swatches, the WATS line, the cunningly refurbished pressed-tin ceiling all look so . . . permanent.

When I head up the street again, the snow is lying sullenly on the sidewalks, and the long, low whistle of a Burlington Northern freight fills the frigid air. Not wanting to, I still think of gold-rush towns like Helena and Deadwood a hundred and twenty years before, and of their hand-painted bathtubs and magnums of champagne, the red-velvet opera houses and mahogany parlor organs, the French and deportment tutors for the newly wealthy miners' children. Ahead of me the airport mesa rises, wind-scoured ochre under an aluminum sky, and beyond it, the Great Plains. Some days, especially in winter, prairie can look hungry, but this is too pretty a day. Waiting, maybe.

The Poppers and the chinook arrive together, the warm, westerly winter wind pouring over the east slope of the Rockies, raising the temperature in Billings by forty degrees in four hours. Frank and Deborah are looking less tense than on previous trips west; if they are not among friends, at least they trust they will not be noisily attacked. Quiet attacks are more the Harvard tradition, and the Harvard Club of Montana has invited the Poppers to speak at a Billings symposium on the future of the Northern Plains.

Montana has always had stronger Eastern connections than other Plains states. Generations of asthmatic or otherwise delicate city children, some of them du Ponts and Rockefellers, were sent here with their governesses for the healthy air, and over the decades many returned, or told their friends.

Francis Blake, Harvard '61, is the club president. He is a rancher in Big Timber (pop. 1,690), in the foothills of the Rockies, and runs an operation large enough to be listed in Dun and Bradstreet's Million Dollar Directory. His Big Timber neighbors have recently included the retired CEO of Levi Strauss, the CEO of Cargill Inc., the fashion photographer Bruce Weber, and California postmodernist architect Frank Gehry. One town over, the landowners (some with working

147

ranches, some with recreational spreads) include a Standard Oil heiress and the actors Dennis Quaid, Jeff Bridges, and Peter Fonda; two towns over are the Sun Oil heir and Ted Turner's 120,000 acres.

Hannibal Anderson, the symposium's moderator—sent from Gardiner, Montana, to Exeter and Harvard—confesses it has been hard to get people to appear on the same panel with the Poppers. The lecture committee ended up with a Princeton economics Ph.D. (who has missed his plane from Missoula) and one family-farm activist, who wanted to know if the club intended to pay the Poppers' way west. "I can't imagine why you would; they're blasphemers!" she protested.

As the auditorium at Rocky Mountain College fills with chat, the accents are Midwest and Cambridge as well as Northern Plains. The Harvard Club of Montana is boots and jeans from the waist down, distinctly tweedy from the waist up. A high school teacher from nearby Red Lodge tells me she has doubts about the Poppers' depopulation figures; in the last ten years she has seen increasing numbers of people coming into the state, not leaving it.

"They come to ski and want to stay, so they try to make a go of some little business, always saying they want to escape the cities. The Californians aren't here yet, thank heavens, but there's a real influx from Minneapolis–St. Paul."

Another Harvard spouse describes how her children deal with their two worlds, East and West. Her son wrote his Yale thesis on his grandfather, a Wall Street banker who came out to Montana in 1894. Her daughter, who had previously scorned Western wear, called home her freshman year with an urgent Ich-Bin-Ein-Montanan shopping list: send boots, denim skirts, and a long cowboy duster to New Haven *immediately*.

I watch the sloping bank of auditorium seats fill with stock-brokers and doctors, ranchers and farmers (Harvard and non-), landscape architects, painters, environmentalists, a rancher/auctioneer (Penn '48), and a dour pair of administrators from the Bureau of Land Management in L.L. Bean sweaters.

It is a room of beautiful sweaters, and beautiful manners. When Deborah's maps go up, the murmurs from Harvardites in bolo ties and local farmers in navy blazers are equally decorous.

"Gracious, that's where *we* live!"

"Four people or fewer: look at that!"

"The Dakotas show up worse than us," observes an elderly rancher with grim satisfaction.

At first the questioning reflects not denial but adaptation. How could people already on the land become the conservators of a Commons, since they know the region best? What about a wheat-and-meat economic conglomerate or cooperative as an alternative to a Buffalo Commons? Land O'Lakes is a cooperative; so are Sunkist and Ocean Spray.

It's been tried in Rapid City, and failed, replies Frank—several cattlemen in the audience loudly confirm this—because Western producers are extremely independent and extremely scattered. The cattlemen seem pleased with this description. The topic of interest rates pleases no one—"The big out-of-state banks aren't sensitive to regional needs!" calls a voice from the crowd—and neither does the issue of Indians.

"The Native Americans often see the Buffalo Commons as a metaphor for a giant white agricultural pullback," explains Frank, and the room is instantly still, but only for an instant.

Then the shouting begins, the questions so fast and angry that the Poppers are getting angry, too. It could be a group therapy session, it could be a town meeting in 1890. This Buffalo

Commons forum is moving from reserve to rage more swiftly than any I have yet seen. The resentments that boil over on this March morning in Billings are the eternal grievances of the American West: paranoia turning to fury at bureaucracy and corporations, at the outsider tourists who would flock to see a Commons. Many in this cement-block hall at Rocky Mountain College have traveled five and six hundred miles from all parts of Montana and Wyoming to inspect Frank and Deborah; what they are hearing impels listener after listener to rise and snarl at a distant and ignorant federal government, and at fancy Eastern professors.

"Well, *really*," mutters a rancher (Harvard '53).

"We don't have tenure in our business," calls a farmer from McCone County, in eastern Montana. "Land is all we have to see us through."

One of the BLM men stands up. "I view with concern your policy agendas. What's your objective? Socialization? Mega-ownership? Eastern control? Didn't you, Professor Popper, once write for *American Land Forum*, which had one of those Communist Rockefellers on its board?"

Frank dramatically slaps his forehead. "Communist Rocke-fellers, huh? Gee, you've seen right through us!" Deborah kicks him.

"We're not doing anything but looking at the numbers," she says as soothingly as possible, but no one wants to be soothed. A moment later she flubs a bit of Montana school-districting ar-cana, and there are cries of "Go back to New Jersey!" "How well do you know this state?" "You're covering up a federal land grab!" and "Why do you want to control us?"

"This recurring talk of plots and secret agendas offends me," Deborah snaps. "We threw out an idea, backed it up, and you refuse to talk about it. Those kinds of questions show a real unwillingness to deal with what you plan to do after you have no topsoil and no water and no towns."

A stocky woman in the front row stands up, brandishing a satin warm-up jacket with a massive anti–Buffalo Commons logo on the back: a buffalo covered by a red circle and slash.

"From Scobey to Ekalaka, we're trying to change things," the woman shouts, addressing not Deborah but the audience. She is Joyce Almy, the organizer of an economic self-help group in eastern Montana that is trying to bring industrial parks and home-based employment to some of the most distressed counties in the state.

"Let's not shoot the messengers!" she beseeches the crowd. "Our children *are* leaving, with joy or reluctance, but they're leaving. If the Poppers are trying to warn us, we'd better listen!"

"Agriculture is not an extractive industry!" shoots back rancher Lyle Quick. "We have to prove to the country that we're good stewards, we have to make peace with the environmentalists, or they'll kill us all!"

"Kill the world, too," says a Wyoming rancher beside me, sullenly. Frank tries to restore peace by explaining, a risky move.

"At the heart of the nation's Western land policy is a conceptual and emotional void that has existed for over a century. The old nineteenth-century rationales—expansion, settlement, defense, economic development—no longer apply. On the political level, environmentalists and developers debate much as they did in 1910. Each side treats the land as a trophy to be withheld from the other. And generations of mutual suspicion, exaggerated claims, and lack of fresh input haven't helped. Deborah and I really do see the Commons as a positive way out of this fruitless, obstructionist, outmoded impasse from which we need—somehow—to extract hope.''

"You can get killed by hope," says Joyce Almy, folding away her anti-Buffalo Commons warm-up jacket.

The next afternoon, the Poppers and I drive to Red Lodge, at the edge of the Beartooth Mountains, the back road into Yellowstone, knowing as we do so that all entrances to the park are iffy this time of year. On the way south, Deborah reads aloud the *Billings Gazette* account of their talk.

" 'Buffalo Refuge Idea Blasted.' Hmmm."

She skips down the page.

"I may have 'flecks of gray in short dark curls,' " says Deborah smugly, "but at least I'm not described as 'a slightly portly Rutgers professor.' "

Why, I ask her, was the Billings forum so fierce?

"Because Montana is already engaged in debate about its future, in some odd way. In Nebraska, in Oklahoma, there was enormous anger and denial, but not the accompanying push and ferment of Montana. Billings is the power center up here. These people are already struggling for turf in the revised West."

At Red Lodge we find a wall of snow. Behind it, in Yellowstone's two-million-acre fastness, three thousand buffalo are roaming, the last wild free-ranging herd in America, their dense winter pelts of bright tan and burnt sienna the only warm notes against the mist and steam rising from hot springs, the snow-heavy pine trees casting long blue shadows, the mountainsides like folded white drapery, the glittering peaks. The Poppers and I have seen the Yellowstone buffalo herds thus, other years, other winters, but today the buffalo are blocked from human curiosity by an eleven-thousand-foot mountain range and a thirty-foot snowpack.

We turn away from Beartooth Pass and head back to Billings through slate and amber fields, the snowy mountains receding behind.

On the plane back to Denver I sit beside a rancher and a sugar beet farmer. All the way across northeast Colorado we look out the window in silence. Like smoke from a hundred prairie fires, mile-high plumes of thin, dry dirt are rising in the golden afternoon light. The dust plumes are shortgrass topsoil, released by the spring tilling, blowing east and away.

"Hate to see the dust rising this early," says the rancher with a sly sideways glance at his seatmate. "Shouldn't ever have broke the sod in the first place." The farmer flushes, turns abruptly from the window, and buries his nose in *Forbes*.

In Colorado alone nearly 750,000 acres of marginal grasslands were plowed between 1978 and 1987, in the interests of efficient, fencepost-to-fencepost crops. In 1989, after 10,000 acres of nearby range were plowed up for planting, one ranch owner in the terrain below us saw flying topsoil bury her grazing land up to the fencetops. Her neighbor called it an act of God. The rancher sued, saying, "It's not an act of God. It's an act of greed. God doesn't have a plow."

Exactly what an acre of Buffalo Commons will look like has always been the weakest point in the Poppers' proposal. It is one thing to divert the Harvard Club of Montana with visions of galloping buffalo; quite another to convince working scientists that a Commons can, or should, be anything more than a metaphor for land-use change.

Carefully worded expressions of confidence that buffalo can coexist with a changing frontier have so far staved off a detailed reckoning, though Frank likes to speculate on the forms of ecotourism a Commons might yield: bison-spotting expeditions; wildlife photo safaris; ghost town tours; tribal buffalo dances and historic parks; buffalo hunts (as the herds grow, and need pruning); even living museums where visitors inspect, Colonial Williamsburg–style, re-creations of a western Kansas wheat farm circa 1990, a North Texas ranch circa 1920, a Lakota village circa 1870. But as the Commons idea disseminates, pressure from scientists for detail increases. The Poppers' vision of one future for the American West is insisting on turning real. Now everyone wants answers, the wildlife biologists especially.

The idea of a Commons leaves range and wildlife ecologists intensely interested, and intensely agitated. Dick Hart, a government biologist from Wyoming, calls the Poppers once they are back at Rutgers, wanting to chew over the problem of top predators. On a Commons, who will eat whom? Buffalo are herbivores; do the Poppers plan to reintroduce the grizzly bear to the Plains? The great gray buffalo wolf, terror of early travelers? What about the mountain lion? And have they thought much about accident coverage?

"Japanese tourists have no fear of large mammals," Hart tells me later. "The Buffalo Commons will need a lot of liability insurance, especially at calving time and when the bulls are in rut. Buffalo don't know their own strength."

When buffalo become imprinted on humans, he adds, they get playful. When they become irritable, some like to attack cars. And they can be prodigiously messy neighbors.

"Just check the accounts of Zebulon Pike and of Lewis and Clark on the environmental degradation caused by a buffalo herd moving through." Hart thinks a minute.

"Also, buffalo are no fools. They dislike degraded land as

much as the next ungulate, and would probably try to migrate onto good range still under private ownership."

To Frank's surprise, Deborah agrees. She has begun tinkering with the scope of the Buffalo Commons. The Poppers' all-Plains map of severe land-use distress is far from monolithic—a county here, six counties there. Consolidation, Deborah thinks, may be in order.

"Aren't we downgrading the Buffalo Commons from the start, by restricting it to marginal or replacement use?" she demands of Frank one day, as they walk from her computer lab to his office. It is only partly a rhetorical question.

"Because if we are," she continues, "that's akin to assuming New Jersey farmland is automatically second-rate; that the Garden State's real purpose now is growing suburbs. The quarter of the Plains we singled out for the Commons is, by definition, second-choice land, stretches of country that just aren't making it under any conditions. Setting up a stable ecological unit can't be done by county lines. We may well have to arrange land uses on a Commons to include more than just the worst and poorest land."

Frank looks at her, alarmed. "What happened to free-market desertion?"

Deborah stands aside to let him enter his buffalo-dotted cubicle. "Dear, we do have to consider connector lands, probably with government buyouts. Otherwise the buffalo will have an awfully hard time roaming. I told you that weeks ago, don't you remember?"

"I guess this will teach me," says Frank, gazing at the land-use map by his desk, frantically recalculating acreages, "to keep my ears open at dinner."

The next week they are featured speakers at a Rutgers ecology department forum. The ecologists argue about predators, press the Poppers for prairie reseeding schedules, and gossip about the conspicuous absence of a visiting ecologist from Kansas, who has refused to attend because he wants no truck with what he calls "national redlining."

But the specificity of the questioning at the forum starts Deborah thinking again, and Frank, too. Always before they have struggled against the hostility and disbelief of Plains citizens, or dealt with relatively large, yes-or-no questions about the shape of a Commons from people outside the academy. "Why should this be done?" is a question the Poppers answer with increasing confidence. "Can it be done?" is another problem entirely.

If a Buffalo Commons ever attempts the leap from hypothetical construct to reality, the earth scientists—biologists, botanists, agronomists, soil specialists, ecologists—will have to design and manage it. In late April an apprehensive Frank Popper stands in a cavernous hotel ballroom, four miles from O'Hare Airport and just over a hundred miles from the muddy banks of the Illinois River where in 1679 Father Louis Hennepin became one of the first Europeans to see an American buffalo, which he promptly shot.

Frank is in Chicago because he is presenting the Buffalo Commons idea to four hundred members of the Society for Ecological Restoration. Deborah has declined the trip and is traveling instead with her son and his swim team to Canton, Ohio, for the week-long national competitions, taking along a stock of Howlin' Wolf tapes and a pile of geography exams to correct. In the bleachers, sitting behind a team from South Dakota, she hides her name badge, not wanting to be thrown into the pool.

While Frank is pleased that those who think about environmental restoration for a living have invited him to address their international conference, the occasion is making him extremely nervous. Ted Sudia, the senior scientist at the National Park Service, has warned him about this crowd.

"Those people don't talk baseball, women, or novels," Sudia cautioned. "They talk restoration. They think restoration. They live for restoration. It's all they do."

Sudia's analysis is borne out by the program, which features papers on "Managing for Pink Milkwort in a Mesic Sand Prairie," "Restoring Coastal Sage Scrub at San Onofre State Beach," "The Role of Alien Vine Control in Piedmont Forests," and "Restoration of a Placer-Mined Subalpine Riparian Ecosystem."

The Society membership includes fifty-odd private restoration firms and consultants; numerous decision-makers at federal, state, and local departments of natural resources, parks, and transportation; a welter of conservation-group representatives and environmental lobbyists; and lots of academics—conservation biologists, environmental-law professors, botanists of wetlands, and botanists of prairie. Between paper sessions the conversation in the halls, unsmiling and intense, is of legislation and logistics, feasibility and costs.

Frank, pale and subdued, roams the lobby before his talk, a social scientist adrift among hard scientists. Restoration ecologists tend to work small, rebuilding a watershed here, a dune system or roadside-vegetation community there. He is afraid they will read a Buffalo Commons as ecological overreaching. Finally he consents to sit in the hotel coffee shop; he picks at a waffle, head bent under the spring evening light that floods from a high rectangular window onto the table. On the vinyl

banquette opposite is the Native American activist Vine Deloria, Jr.—sturdy, graying, and a practiced provocateur in the
cause of the Plains. Deloria is trying to cheer Frank up.

"It's brilliant! The Buffalo Commons is the best idea I've
heard in years," Deloria says, attacking a plate of barbecued ribs.
He is all for the Poppers' project. So, he assures Frank, are most
of the Great Plains' original tenants.

"As you might imagine," he adds, "your research has major
implications for tribal land claims. We're trying right now to get
back eleven thousand acres of the Black Hills. So the Commons
has us very, *very* interested."

The author of *Custer Died for Your Sins*, an Episcopalian
theologian, an attorney, and a Standing Rock Sioux, Deloria
currently works at the University of Colorado's Center for
Studies of Ethnicity and Race in America. Though he mostly
teaches seminars in Native American thought, he retains a
lawyerly pleasure in argument. At power dinner parties throughout the West, Deloria's jovial discourse drives water developers
and investment bankers crazy by the time the soup course is
cleared. To every impassioned outpouring over the ultimate
morality and immediate practicality of saving small Plains towns
and farms, Deloria says only, So?

But the ranchers and the farmers will be forced to sell out,
someone usually retorts, and then they'll have to go to work in
Omaha electronics factories, or open bed-and-breakfasts.

So?

But we can't let ourselves be pushed around by theorists, or by
the Feds. What do they know? We're talking ancestral land here.

Did you say "ancestral"? Deloria will inquire, all courtly
amiability. What an *interesting* word to choose. ("If we have to
give Rapid City back to the Sioux, I'll know just who to blame,"

a South Dakota lawyer told me once, his voice half bitter, half admiring.)

At the Society for Ecological Restoration, Vine Deloria is on the program just before Frank Popper. He talks of the spiritual dimensions of ecological restoration, and of restoration as a scientific practice that remains necessarily attuned to the spirit of place. From the viewpoint of Native American tradition, he tells them, the Great Plains is not at all the blank white barrenness depicted in nineteenth-century atlases, but rather a tapestry of neutral places and benevolent places, habitable places and places to be avoided.

This intense geographical awareness is accompanied by a ceremonial disposition of species. Plants, mammals, birds, and reptiles, like humans, are all members of the society of place. Unlike humans they are also bearers of messages, intermediaries between worlds invisible and visible.

"The Plains," Deloria continues, "were and are a covenant between human and bison. Our bones go back to the ground to become the dust that nourishes the grasses that feed the buffalo."

Vine Deloria also issues a warning.

"Don't romanticize us. Indians have an extensive and specific technical knowledge of Plains survival, as well as an extensive and specific spiritual tradition. If you have the nerve, I suggest you take both into account. After all, you people have been on the Great Plains for two hundred years. We've been there for forty thousand."

Frank's turn. As he stands to speak, I realize that this is the first conference in a long time in which no television lights and no photographers are in evidence. It is just as well. This is not a camera-friendly audience. In McCook, Nebraska, as in Oklahoma City, Frank Popper was cast as a radical doomsayer before he uttered a word. At the Denver planning-convention debate, and to some extent in Billings, he was presumed guilty of undermining economic development and the booster spirit that argues for progress at any price. Here in Chicago the response is no response. The restoration scientists listen to him with blank, set faces, arms crossed over plaid workshirts, their extremely sensible shoes planted firmly and wide apart on the ballroom floor. A few of the men finger beards; a few of the women (the gender ratio is about eight to one, male-female) smooth their denim skirts. But in the aggregate they are about as expressive as a roomful of Egyptian statuary. The only evident emotion is impatience. As soon as the discussion period begins I find out why. They outstrip even Frank in eagerness to see the Great Plains that might have been.

"I'm sorry, but Popper's way too conservative," an agronomist employed by the state of California announces under the roar of speculation that follows the close of the Popper talk. He is frowning with disappointment, fingers tapping corduroyed knees. "For starters, we need to give Kansas back to the buffalo."

A botanist from Topeka and I look at him, ready to laugh understandingly, but he is not in a joking mood.

"The settlement of the Plains was soil murder. Everyone has always known that land so arid is basically meant for buffalo. Right from the start they've known it—Lewis and Clark, Gilpin, Powell—and the agribusiness companies and the fertilizer and pesticide manufacturers all know it, too."

He rises and stalks off toward the exhibit area. He is one of very few to leave the hall once Frank stops speaking. The rest are far too engrossed. A dozen variants and visions of a Commons are floated, examined, shot down, applauded. It is intellectual play, but the sort that could change the face of a continent. Frank is glowing.

"Eventually," he confides to the crowd, "the Commons may be the world's largest historic-preservation project."

Deloria is asked his views on natural predators.

"I prefer wolves and coyotes to bankers and lawyers," he replies. Some of the scientists—mostly those holding large corporate and federal grants—murmur angrily. Others cheer.

Al Steuter, the Nature Conservancy manager from the Niobrara Valley Preserve in the Nebraska Sand Hills, where a herd of four hundred buffalo has been maintained since 1985, explains that a buffalo herd is like an amoeba, intensely social.

"If the Commons is instituted, how will the buffalo herds cross an interstate?" asks a botanist from Pennsylvania.

"Any way they want to," a Texas biologist calls out.

"We've considered that, actually," says Frank Popper, pleased. "In thirty or forty years the herds will doubtless be up to five or six figures. A system of helicopter spotters could track the roaming buffalo and make road announcements, as happens now for heavy rain or snow: 'I-80 closed Monday due to buffalo crossings.' A system of buffalo underpasses and overpasses would help too."

Excited talk of similar massive restorations for other American regions begins to build. All over the room people are scribbling down references, noting names of project leaders and funding sources. Some in the crowd rise to remind the group of current efforts to reintroduce caribou to the tamarack swamps and conifer forests of upper Minnesota. Other ecologists cite the need to reestablish some of the great Southern wetlands lost to industrial and urban sprawl since World War II—at this, many people nod—and still others want to explain plans to restore native chaparral in and around Los Angeles.

Restoration hot-spots currently include the California coast, Florida (where wetlands loss and phosphate mining keep restorationists on the run), and the Midwest, especially the Chicago-Madison axis. In New England, mitigating environmental damage has been pursued more than full-scale habitat re-creation. However, Maine is named repeatedly as a potential forest-restoration site, and most in the audience nod again, vigorously.

"In 1895," Frank observes, "most of primeval New England had been clear-cut and burnt over. It was a disaster area of erosion and stumps achieved at backbreaking human cost. A prediction that the great forests of New England would return as second-growth woodlands would have seemed insane. And if anyone *had* believed you, reforestation would have been called 'anti-progress,' as odd as wanting the buffalo back on the Plains. But more of New England is now covered by trees than at any time since the Pilgrims arrived."

At 11:00 P.M., long after the session's official close, dozens of restorationists continue to mill about the half-darkened ballroom, trading ideas on Great Plains re-creation. Like the early moonshot scientists, shown a goal and told to make it happen, they are entranced with possibility. Still, the logistics of earth-keeping are complicated in the extreme. Frank Popper listens, head whipping like a Wimbledon spectator, as the language of specialists surges around him.

They argue soil preparation and seed harvesting and seed mixes; do battle over no-till planting versus successional planting; debate chemical weed control versus prairie burning. They assess predator balances and the demography of microsites; caution one another about optimum grass:forb ratios and distribution of ant species; factor in the mysteries of black-footed ferret mating patterns and the five best ways to monitor microbial biomass in the shortgrass prairie.

Always the talk is of managing, managing, and more managing. Tallgrass, midgrass, or shortgrass, the prairie cannot come back by itself, not anymore. The original biospheric net was too intricate; the damage is too great. And this crowd wants not a modest rehabilitation, or even sample acreage for exhibition, but re-creation of the Great Plains grasslands in all their presettlement glory, Texas to Montana, the 98th meridian to the front range of the Rockies. After fifteen minutes of listening to methodological infighting, Frank Popper moves away and sits, forgotten, on the edge of the speakers' platform, watching the intent faces, thinking over the power of metaphor.

"Planners and geographers must deal in metaphor constantly," he reflects, "but scientists, farm-country people, and wheeler-dealers are powerfully resistant to the sort of historical double vision a Commons requires. Yet once they shake loose from their ruts, mental and emotional—if they can shake loose—anything is possible. Even Deborah and me."

With Vine Deloria and the natural-history writer Barry Lopez, he sits up late in the hotel lounge, talking buffalo. Deloria tells Frank that the Poppers have all the young Indians politicized. Frank blanches. "Great; we'll be responsible if some rancher gets scalped."

All three have felt the burdens of eco-fame. "If I have to go to another tribal war dance I'll scream," Deloria says. Lopez, who teaches occasionally at Notre Dame but lives and writes in Oregon, describes the trials of being typecast as an eco-guru.

But mostly Frank Popper, Vine Deloria, and Barry Lopez tell

Wes Jackson stories. Jackson, a plant geneticist, will arrive at the Chicago meeting two days hence. Everyone on the enviro-circuit knows Jackson. He and his wife, Dana, have spent fifteen shoestring years at their Land Institute in Salina, Kansas, asking the prairie to yield its polycultural secrets. Conventional farming intimidates the land into productivity. The Jacksons would prefer to persuade; they focus their research on sustainable agriculture. Their experiments with prairie plant genetics, in hopes of producing commercially viable perennial crops, represent the longest of long shots. One or more tries may pan out in ten years, or fifty, or a hundred. No one knows.

Instead of taking land out of production, as Bret Wallach or the Poppers suggest, the Jacksons and their staff are trying to find alternatives to planting wheat or corn on Plains land that is erosion-prone or semiarid. Achieving a winter-hardy sorghum would be a start, or a grama grass that keeps its edible seed heads intact until harvest. As the aquifer drops and the topsoil blows, the Jacksons are attracting more and more interest, even among farmers who once viewed sustainable agriculture as a near-obscenity but now keep an anxious eye on reports out of Salina, hoping for a plant-genetics breakthrough that will allow them to stay in business and on the land.

When Frank Popper returns from the Chicago meeting, he retrieves from his paper piles, then rereads, slowly, a letter sent him by Wes Jackson a few months before.

"When I was a kid there were no deer around in Kansas," Jackson wrote. "Ten years ago I had never seen a turkey. Now I see deer every day, and twenty wild turkeys roost in my woods a quarter-mile south. Thirteen half-grown turkeys walked by my window through the herbary late this summer. We are beginning to welcome the animals back, the wild ones we wiped out during colonization, and if we are truly to discover America, we will have to accept much of the original back. I was initially taken aback by the Buffalo Commons. I still don't know if it is the very best plan, but I have no other alternative to suggest after the extractive economy comes to an end."

After the restoration-ecology meeting I visit the University of Wisconsin Arboretum in Madison, Wisconsin, to talk more about prairies with William Jordan III, one of the Society's original organizers. This twelve-hundred-acre preserve—half open-air research laboratory, half miniature wilderness—is separated from the city only by the curving shore of Lake Wingra on the north and the eight-lane Beltline highway on the south. To reach Jordan's office I decide to leave the winding paved road and shortcut over on foot, through the heart of the painstakingly restored late-spring prairie.

A hundred and fifty feet from the tarmac I find myself a hundred and fifty years in the past. Warblers dart along the tops of the grasses, chasing lunch. The prairie is just completing its first-stage blossoming. I walk knee-deep, then waist-deep, in blowing grasses—pale green, pale gold. But most of the action is at ankle level, where pastel flowers crowd in among the grass stems: pale-violet lupine, the streamlined white of shooting star, the flat pink of phlox, the twining sea-anemone clusters, rose and gold, of prairie smoke. July and August will intensify the prairie palette, bringing the deep oranges and fire-reds of Indian blanket and butterfly weed, the pale-gold pyramids of evening primrose, the bobbing swaths of black-eyed Susans.

A cornfield or a wheatfield is a serious place, as single-minded as an engine climbing a long grade. If cultivated prairie land is a factory, this is a festival. Bands of moving air, here cool, there warm, flow above the prairie floor like currents in the ocean. A delicious smell, like wind-dried laundry, rises each time I step on the sun-warmed mat of last year's grasses, now settling to straw, and that scent is in turn overlaid by the wild, acrid saps from leaves and stems that will never know an herbicide, or a blade.

I brush past a stand of thigh-high plants, plain and strong, the hairy edges of their long lobed leaves turning to the late-morning sun. This is compass plant, or cutleaf silphium, and by July it will be six feet tall, topped with a many-petaled yellow flower the size of a saucer. When I was nine or ten and roaming the Curtis Prairie and the Arboretum's marshes and hardwood forests every summer day (Madison was a smaller place then, and safer), I liked to sit beneath the compass plant canopy, among the forest of stems, and watch the clear light move over the crowding petals above me, flicking them into maize and buttercup and bronze.

Early travelers in Wisconsin reported that the golden silphiums and other summer prairie growth could rise shoulder-high to a man on horseback, the stems so resilient that when buffalo roved the tallgrass prairie, the swaths of grasses trampled by the animals would spring up again and close behind the herd even as they passed. (The eastern range of the Plains buffalo in the eighteenth century included Wisconsin, but by the 1830s, though the silphium remained for a time, the buffalo had already retreated back across the Mississippi.)

The University of Wisconsin Arboretum, with its shortgrass and tallgrass prairies, was invented in 1934 largely through the urgings of Aldo Leopold, a Yale-trained professor of wildlife management interested in the infant discipline of restoration and the hope it offered ecosystems battered by depression and the Dust Bowl.

Much 1930s conservation work was rehabilitative, rather like refurbishing a colonial mansion with an eye to contemporary comforts (microwave ovens concealed behind the paneling, an electric blanket on the canopied four-poster). Re-creation re-creates. Virgin prairie and oak savannah in the 1830s, a stretch of overgrazed and degraded farm pasture by the 1930s, Madison's Curtis Prairie is the earliest large-scale effort to reproduce midcontinent nature as it was when the first settlers arrived.

Or nearly so. "What a thousand acres of Silphiums looked like when they tickled the bellies of the buffalo is a question never again to be answered, and perhaps not even asked," wrote Leopold later in *A Sand County Almanac*.

William Jordan—once I forge through the last ranks of grasses to his Arboretum office—shares some of Leopold's caution. Tall and lanky, his narrow face is watchful until he warms to his subject, the history and practice of prairie-saving.

"You restore a prairie for love, not money," Jordan tells me. Prairies, unlike wetlands, he explains, are not protected by legislation; an acre of tallgrass prairie is not nearly as economically valuable as an acre of corn. From a horticultural point of view a prairie is a high-maintenance proposition, basically a giant herbaceous garden border requiring active intervention.

We walk outdoors under a clear noon sky, the roar of the Beltline highway, half a mile away, very loud today through the tall intervening stands of pine. Leopold predicted the Beltline's coming and talked a reluctant legislature and board of regents into investing in worn-out land for scientific restoration at a time when no one believed that Madison would stretch much beyond its 1930s bounds. Now development has completely encircled the Arboretum's preserve and reaches fifteen miles beyond.

The least sentimental of land scientists, Leopold still hoped to teach a land ethic. Think like a mountain, he urged. Country-side can carry a cultural harvest as well as a per-acre yield. Land is both community and commodity. In the upper Midwest, thanks largely to the land-grant universities and their extension services, Leopold's ideas have had clear and lasting effect. Farmers whose parents and grandparents resisted and denied all change are now much more alert to innovation, from introduc-ing new crops to endorsing erosion-control plowing. That land stewardship is also sound business practice has become widely understood in agricultural states like Minnesota, Wisconsin, and Michigan.

Still, a reliable water table and a varied state economy permit the luxury of experimentation. On the waterless Plains one wrong move can bankrupt, and innovation is full of wrong moves. Understanding too much is not always desirable. Under-standing might lead to doubt; doubt, to change. Suffering seems easier, sometimes. Besides, it ennobles. ("I always worked till I was ready to drop at the end of each day so I didn't *have* to think," my Pierre grandmother once told me, explaining eighty years on the Plains. "When people asked what I was giving up for Lent, I would tell them: Not a thing. Our entire *lives* have been Lent.")

Restoration on the Great Plains, says William Jordan, walking past Leopold's prairie, glorious in the May morning, is hard to get discussed. Across the Missouri the taboos against admission of wrongheadedness are very strong, and so is belief in the technological fix. More and meaner herbicides. Salvation by genetic engineering. Piping Great Lakes water a thousand miles southwest to drench carrot fields in arid Kansas. The sciences that should be allies of prairie restoration, like range manage-ment, are ostensibly close in purpose but a long way off in spirit; even further off in practice.

Besides, in restoration, scale is crucial. The Curtis Prairie, only three hundred acres wide, was assembled like a labor-intensive jigsaw, using sods from relic Wisconsin prairies. Other restorations have used scroungings from cemeteries and roadsides. You can start a prairie with nursery plants, or with seed planted broadcast-fashion.

"At the Morton Arboretum in Chicago they have redone four or five acres in meticulous horticultural style," Jordan explains, "planting specimens at twelve-inch intervals and weeding the whole thing on hands and knees with linoleum knives. Using salt spreaders to plant seeds, six hundred acres of prairie have been restored at Fermilab, near Chicago, complete with buffalo."

Techniques for even larger-scale work exist. You can start with a few species, then add more, and still more, until a full successional restoration is reached. Or you can restore in strips, hoping that the prairie plants will seed themselves, bleeding outward like madras.

All agriculture and horticulture, Jordan reminds me, is an imitation of nature, more or less abstract, more or less stylized. In the case of the American prairies, traditional Plains agriculture has tried to erase the picture entirely and draw a new one. The Poppers, he hopes (as is indeed the case), will settle for a pretty fair reproduction of the original, on an enormous scale. The actual restorations attempted to date, the Curtis Prairie included, have demanded an exact copy—an instinct for historical correctness like that which drove Germany to rebuild entire medieval and Renaissance cities, stone by stone, after World War II.

There is, Jordan notes, much we need to know, much we have forgotten, much we never knew. When making a Buffalo Commons, do you simply pull cattle off and put buffalo on? Which native plant species are the most depleted? Which best sustained the buffalo in the first place? Yes, American ecology grew from the study of lakes and of prairies; yes, prairie study lies at the heart of our national environmental awareness; but restoring a fifth of the United States is not a project for well-intentioned civic groups with trowels.

He does, however, cite the Kentucky farmer and writer Wendell Berry. " 'In plowing under the prairies, we did not know what we were doing because we did not know what we were undoing. In restoring damaged land, we learn to heal ourselves.' "

When I get back to Manhattan, arriving in midafternoon in midtown on the La Guardia Carey bus, the island is deep in gridlock. I realize I have already missed my train, the local out of Penn Station—NewYorkNewarkElizabethLindenRahwayMetroparkMetuchenEdisonNewBrunswickJerseyAvenuePrincetonJunction(changeforPrinceton)Trenton. I use my unwanted leisure to detour through Grand Central Station and out the other side, walking up Park Avenue and across to Madison. It is a day of pale spring sun, and within their protective wrought-iron fencing the ailanthus and callery pear trees are lifting green branches skyward along every side street, defying the perpetual shadows cast by the Manhattan skyline, which turns denser year by year.

The torrent of moving bodies stalls a few yards ahead. I crane to learn the cause but spot only a crowd in front of an expensive East Side florist's shop. They are cooing—"Oooh!" "Awwww!"—a reaction so exotic in these parts that I edge through, suitcase and all, to find the cause.

A redheaded employee in a white florist's smock is standing by a Palladian-arched door, her arms full of prairie. The shop is selling personal prairies for fifty dollars—a seven-by-eighteen-inch weathered white-cedar box included, delivery extra. The New Yorkers are riveted.

"Pretty!" says a splendidly barbered executive. He tucks a slim leather briefcase between his tailored knees and, driven by some atavistic impulse, lightly brushes his hand across and across its vigorous green crown. The wheatgrass stems, looking succulent enough for the fussiest ungulate, bend in a blast of diesel from an uptown bus.

"Don't *touch*, sir," says the clerk. "Our prairies last for weeks if you give them water, but they sulk if you pick at them." He snatches his hand away.

On an impulse, even though it is almost rush hour, I find a cab and travel, slowly, down to the gallery district, SoHo, heading for the Dia Art Foundation and its permanent installation on Wooster Street called the New York Earth Room. The exhibition space is suffused in silence, or almost-silence; the taxi horns and city roar suddenly sound very far away. The Earth Room is just that, white walls and track lighting and ceiling columns—a classic SoHo art-display space, only this one is filled with topsoil.

"So pure," says a girl beside me wearing four earrings, black leggings, and a long black T-shirt. She inhales, and her eyes close reverently. The dirt covers the whole room, neatly raked, knee-deep. Canadian dirt, says the brochure, but in the middle of Manhattan it hardly seems to matter. The fourteen tons of dark mollisol smell rich and fresh, like the new-turned Kansas fields of Kenny MacDonald.

A few days later the U.S. Soil and Conservation Service reports that more than 14 million acres on the Great Plains have been damaged by wind erosion alone since the previous

November—the worst damage since record-keeping began in 1954. Reported damaged in November and December 1990 were 1,844,437 acres, up from 1,743,000 acres in the same two months of 1989.

I try to call Kenny MacDonald and the Fries family, to see how they are getting along in the drought. It is just a year since Jeffrey Aaronson and I stood in their fields and watched the spring plowing for wheat. The Kansas operator searches her computer, then tries all the little towns nearby, but cannot find a phone listing. "Must have moved away," she says at last.

The Poppers' in-box continues to fill. A *Congressional Quarterly* article, part of an issue on the continuing decline of rural America, covers the Commons proposal in numbing detail, emphasizing the procedural snarls that have held in limbo all legislation to alter delivery of federal aid to rural areas. The Bush administration's extreme reluctance to become more involved in rural development assistance, plus the budget deficit, are considered by all involved the two largest obstacles to farm-country aid increases. The former may change in some future election; the latter will probably be a permanent roadblock to federal bailouts of American farming.

A U.S. Department of Agriculture study called "The Big Meadow" is released, pointing out that many of the farmers who own Great Plains land are actually living in other states—nice green ones, like Missouri or Iowa—and flying in to keep tabs on their Plains holdings, a high-tech, twenty-first-century version of suitcase farming. Another USDA study announces in the British journal *Nature* that global warming may be tied to the intensive use of nitrogen fertilizers in cultivation of shortgrass prairie.

The USDA's Economic Research Service brings out a rush assessment of the Buffalo Commons proposal at the request of one of the department's undersecretaries, who read about the Commons in a Midwestern newspaper and wants the research staff to tell him *right away* if bringing back the buffalo to the American prairies is feasible.

The Poppers are sent a bootleg copy of the report and pronounce it full of biological and stylistic infelicities—"They say we're going to uproot one million people!" cries Frank, outraged, flipping pages. "We've never, ever said that."

Still, the government is clearly paying attention to the Poppers and their ideas. Perhaps too much so. A far larger USDA study of the Commons, the Poppers learn, is under way in Washington. Frank fires off a letter, offering access to all their research files and statistical compilations, but he never hears back.

In the meantime Deborah repaints the living room in mango, in honor of spring and in honor of her new self-declared persona as Mother Earth; a comfortable step up, she feels, from her former incarnation as the enigmatic Mona Lisa of Land Use, who ran the overhead projector but let Frank do most of the talking. Frank has begun answering his Rutgers office phone "Hello, Buffalo Central," but Deborah makes him stop. Undaunted, he invents a political action committee, PopperPAC ("Dial 1-900-BUFFALO"), and wonders if the two of them could start a sideline in guaranteed-to-backfire endorsements of candidates running for office in Great Plains states.

Time magazine's Chicago bureau calls, to discuss a follow-up feature on the Poppers and the West. National Public Radio's *Weekend Edition* schedules a taping. There is a definite cottage industry now of wholly or partly anti-Popper studies: one done at Nebraska Wesleyan University, another ("North Dakota 2000") contracted by that state to the Stanford Research Institute. In Denver, Phil Burgess of the Center for the New West—who has lost few chances throughout the fall and winter to opine, at planning and Western-history conferences, that Frank and Deborah are a menace to the Plains—announces that his think tank has received a Ford Foundation grant to underwrite a three-year study ("A New Vision of the Heartland: The Great Plains in Transition") to prove, among other things, that the Buffalo Commons is a dangerous fallacy. A graduate student in the University of Minnesota's geography department writes to inform them that he is composing a research paper on the Buffalo Commons phenomenon. Nicholas Popper, with eighth-grade practicality, suggests renaming the whole Buffalo Commons project. "Elk are very nonthreatening," he assures his parents. "Call it the Elk Estate."

Worried that the maelstrom of publicity will hurt her own dissertation's chances, Deborah labors through the spring to make her examination of stable Plains counties even duller than scholarly convention requires, loading on the bibliography, trying out data packages, regression analyses, chi-squares. "I've never seen a statistic I didn't like," she assures everyone who inquires about her progress. She also briefly considers reverting to Dissertation Plan A, a history of early-nineteenth-century urban-development and banking practices in Paterson, New Jersey.

"Maybe it would be smarter," she says one April afternoon, watching rain fall over the gloomy backyards of Highland Park from her study window, "to research a topic where everyone involved is safely dead."

*   *   *

Late in April the Poppers receive a call from Doug Coffman, an anthropologist and writer in Oregon with an interest in American bison history. Coffman has spent much of the last five years researching the work of the Washington, D.C., taxidermist William Hornaday, who was sent west by the Smithsonian in 1886 to harvest specimens of the nearly extinct buffalo for the museum's collection.

In September of that year Hornaday's party set out from Miles City for the Missouri-Yellowstone divide in search of a remnant herd reported to inhabit the high dry center of Montana, the country traditionally called the Big Open. Ten years before, an estimated half-million bison had grazed this region; Hornaday and his Smithsonian party searched buttes and ravines and badlands for three months, found 35 to 40 buffalo, and killed 24. Their largest quarry, a bull nearly six feet tall and 1,700 pounds, made a lasting impression.

"Thirty yards away from him I pulled up," Hornaday later wrote, "and gazed upon him with genuine astonishment. He seemed to me then . . . the grandest quadruped I ever beheld, lions, tigers and elephants not excepted . . . He seemed to me like the very last one of his race, that he knew it as well as I . . . With the greatest reluctance I ever felt about taking the life of an animal, I shot the noble beast through the lungs . . . and his last breath led me to exclaim fervently, 'Thank heaven! It's over, at last.' "

Hornaday spent the rest of his life working for buffalo preservation, becoming the first president of the American Bison Society in 1905. As head of the New York Zoological Society he helped establish the Wichita Mountains buffalo preserve in Oklahoma, where eighty-five years later the descendants of the bison he sent west eyed Poppers and network cameras with massive equanimity.

Hornaday also wrote *The Extermination of the American Bison*, a classic account of species-extinction. One of his lithographed maps for the book pinpoints areas where the last buffalo held out. The dwindling circles on the page, indicating the shrinkage of these final Great Plains habitats, look like the final puddles of a great drying lake.

On the Northern Plains Hornaday indicates Montana's Big Open, northeast of Billings, as the dwelling-place of the 10 bison he did not kill in 1886. In Yellowstone Park, 200 remained. Twenty-five or so had been reported where Colorado, Oklahoma, and Kansas come together, north and west of present-day Gotebo and Quitaque. Another 20 in Colorado, where the Central Plains and the Rockies meet, a last remnant of the Arkansas herd that once roamed near McCook and Hayes Center.

When Coffman made a plastic overlay of Hornaday's 1889 buffalo-sanctuary map and set it atop the Poppers' distressed-county units of the Buffalo Commons, he found the parallels marvelously, frighteningly precise. When Deborah sees the evidence she is not entirely convinced.

"It's not a *total* match," she says. Frank's taste for historical poetry makes him more sanguine about the discovery.

"Just think, in 1889 Hornaday was sitting in Washington plotting out where the last buffalo were still alive; and a hundred-some years later we're sitting at computers plotting land-use strategies for where the buffalo might be again a generation from now, and some of the answers are the same. History is *real*."

May, cold and wet, creeps over New Brunswick. The lumbering campus buses are packed with damp Rutgers undergraduates brooding about finals. Dogwoods and forsythia shimmer in the morning rain beside the murky Raritan River.

At the urban studies department Frank and Deborah hang slickers and umbrellas to dry, then settle down to scan the latest batch of Commons reportage and commentary from out West. They are so resigned now to being drubbed in print that it takes them a few minutes to register the change in tone. They are being recast in the trans-Mississippi press as subversives no longer, but prophets.

Both Poppers pore over the pages, reading the good parts out loud, then jumping up to photocopy clips and post them on the Buffalo Commons bulletin board, which by now occupies two-thirds of the wall space along the departmental hallway.

"They *like* us!" says Deborah, in a fair Sally Field imitation.

"Aha!" says Frank. "Maybe Sally Field can play you in the movie version of the creation of the Buffalo Commons, not Faye Dunaway. I, of course, will be portrayed by John Travolta or Jack Nicholson, whichever looks better in glasses and a sweater."

He riffles through the stack of newspapers once more, shaking his head.

"Our clippings seem to be encapsulating the entire Elisabeth Kübler-Ross sequence of reactions when faced with death," he says, "all the way from initial denial to anger to depression to bargaining and—not quite yet—acceptance." He is silent a moment. "It's as if Deborah and I are therapists for an entire American region. Except we must convince our patients that beyond the death of the world they know lies rebirth, redemption, resurrection—the first stable, healthy economy the Plains have seen in the white period. We haven't done that yet."

A column in the Grand Island, Nebraska, *Independent*:

What the Poppers are forcing the Plains people to do is take an honest, wide-eyed look at what is actually happening to us living in rural Nebraska. . . . Land is a finite resource, and the Plains will be a Sahara eventually, considering all the bulldozing, leveling, drilling, pumping, draining, scraping, etc. as landowners scheme to add two more rows of irrigated monoculture in a land-abuse policy!

An editorial in the *Tulsa World*:

The Buffalo Commons is not as crazy as it sounds. . . . On some parts of the Plains, the billions spent on farm subsidies might be used more efficiently if the government simply bought the land and let the buffalo roam.

High Country News, Paonia, Colorado:

The West should recognize it is moving away from cowboys and cattle and an indestructible landscape, and toward a fragile, arid land about to be destroyed by those who lived there and those who coveted its resources from afar.

The lead editorial in the *Des Moines Register*:

If the Poppers' estimated time of death for the High Plains is premature, the demise could nevertheless be inevitable, unless its occupants quit their wasteful ways with water. If it comes to a choice of robbing the central states or converting the land to shortgrass and buffalo, logic says bring on the buffalo.

"There's just one problem," says Frank, staring at the bag of buffalo chips on his filing cabinet. "All this madly favorable commentary comes from areas outside the Plains. Des Moines isn't a Plains city. Neither is Tulsa. Grand Island is mostly hog and corn country, just on the east edge of the Plains. Paonia is on the far side of the Rockies. We still haven't heard from the future residents of the bulk of the Buffalo Commons."

But from the deep Plains, Central, Southern, and Northern, there is only silence.

When Deborah studies the preliminary county-level data from the 1990 U.S. Census a few weeks later, she comes running into Frank's office, astounded. The population losses between 1980 and 1990 are far worse than anyone predicted, worse than anyone dreamed. The Plains are hemorrhaging people. West of the 98th meridian, fifty of Nebraska's fifty-two counties lost population in the last decade. So did thirty-eight of North Dakota's western forty-one counties. Twenty-two of Oklahoma's twenty-three. *American Demographics*, using the same data to discuss marketing strategies for the rural parts of Plains and Western states during the last decade of the century, observes there may soon be no one left there to market to.

Frank and Deborah have been devising new ways to keep the left half of the nation mad at them, mostly by continuing to research the phenomenon of the reappearing frontier. Since 1980 the tally of American counties with less than two people per square mile has grown from 143 to 150—"an increase that doesn't sound incredibly impressive," says Frank, "but actually is, since these are big-area counties where desertion is likely only to increase, and more big counties will become frontier in future censuses. The return of the frontier may continue until 2050 or later."

If one defines frontier, as nineteenth-century investigators sometimes did, as a population density not of less than two people per square mile but of less than six, the expanding American frontier looks even more impressive. In that category are 394 counties, all in the West. Together they account for 1.6 million square miles, or 45 percent of the continental United States, on which live just 1 percent of the U.S. population. Six Plains and Western states (Kansas, Nebraska, New Mexico, Oregon, Utah, and Washington) now have congressional districts that are, by these ground rules, heavily frontier. The entire states of Alaska, Montana, the Dakotas, Nevada, Idaho, Utah, and Wyoming are mostly frontier. And all eighteen Western states have many legislative districts that can be defined as frontier.

"Unlike the nineteenth-century version, the twenty-first-century frontier will not be a place to conquer," Frank Popper argues. "We tried that approach to land use, and the resulting economic and water drainage in effect enlarged and intensified frontier conditions. The frontier currently sneaking up on us in the rural West, a county here, a county there, will not be a hinterland to ignore, as it was in the twentieth century." He gnaws on a ballpoint pen, rejects it, tries a pencil.

"And unlike both the nineteenth- and the twentieth-century frontiers," he continues, "Deborah and I think it will be a place where preservation and extraction coexist. Call it the kinder, gentler frontier. Or maybe the end-of-history frontier. If the nation is lucky, it will be the world's first sustainable-development frontier. If we are not lucky, we will create a wasteland for the second time in as many centuries. This last, once-in-history chance to do well by the West is not, perhaps, one we deserve."

All kinds of Western inhabitants, human and otherwise, are changing neighborhoods these days. The Poppers, fascinated, track reports from a West that seems to be turning wilder by the week. Timber wolves, eliminated from the Yellowstone region by ranchers in the 1930s, have been reintroduced to the area. Wolflike, they are killing and devouring not squirrels, not rabbits, but the 450-pound steers that are allowed to graze in the national forests under Interior Department regulations.

More and more hungry buffalo, meanwhile, have been straying beyond their Yellowstone refuge in search of winter fodder. Many are shot on sight as potential brucellosis carriers, in accord with Montana law. The Park Service has tried putting hay out, but the buffalo, with their recolonizing instincts, roam right by it and over the invisible line that transforms them from federally protected animals into disposable state property.

No one is happy with the bison-killing, least of all the Park Service; there have been pointed suggestions from ranchers, hunters, conservation groups, and environmental activists alike that too many buffalo inhabit the park anyway: too many mouths overgrazing, causing soil erosion; too many cloven hooves roiling and muddying the waters of the Yellowstone River, threatening the fish. Is a buffalo more worthy than a trout? Than a tree? The arguments break out all over again.

The course of prairie preservation is no more consistent. Two weeks after the ecological restoration conference in Chicago, conservation volunteers save two acres of virgin Illinois prairie due to become a gravel pit, moving thousands of plants by hand and rerooting them in a preserve six miles away—the first time a chunk of wilderness has ever been physically transplanted on such a scale.

But five months after that the owner of the largest stretch of untouched prairie in northeast Kansas plowed it under, ending two years of negotiation to save the eighty tallgrass acres. A highway bypass is set to go in, several hundred yards away, and additional development with it.

A neighboring farmer said, "I question the wisdom of plowing up good prairie, but I would defend his right to do it. It's his land."

Frank and Deborah continue to think big. They have no choice. Buffalo Commons cousins and spinoffs and parallels seem to be floating everywhere. In the once-lonely landscape of long-range land-use planning for the Plains, the Poppers suddenly have plenty of company.

The Institute for the Rockies, a citizens' group in Hamilton, Montana, continues to propose an East African–style game preserve in the Big Open section of eastern Montana, featuring buffalo, pronghorn, and other indigenous wildlife.

"I'd like to see seventy-five thousand buffalo roaming Montana in my lifetime," says Bob Scott, the idea's progenitor. Local reaction is not enthusiastic. "You may have a revolution on your hands," the mayor of Jordan once told Scott. If a Big Open were instituted, Jordan (pop. 485) would be in its center. The roads that pass through Jordan are the state's least-traveled paved highways, as its residents are quick to tell you, and it is the last town left in Montana to support a public high school dormitory, built in the 1930s for children of ranchers who live beyond the reach of any daily school bus.

Farther south, matters look more promising. The Tulsa office of the Nature Conservancy announces the fifteen-million-dollar establishment of 52,000 Osage County acres in eastern Oklahoma as a tallgrass prairie preserve, the largest preservation project yet, and one that embraces an entire watershed. By 1993 it will be stocked with 3,500 buffalo. The Conservancy plans to manage this land the old-fashioned way, with fire in the form of controlled burn-offs.

The impulse to save ecosystems is not confined to the United States. China, the Poppers learn, has announced the creation of the world's largest wildlife reserve, to protect a Tibetan wilderness the size of Colorado and its various free-roaming inhabitants: antelopes, gazelles, brown bears, and yaks. In Costa Rica a debt-for-nature swap, underwritten by the Swedish government and assorted private philanthropies, will allow that nation to purchase land degraded by farming and ranching. The 200,000 acres are to be restored and managed as native dry tropical forest.

Frank flies to Saskatchewan to speak at a conference and comes home beaming; after years of internecine bickering, provincial government against federal authorities, Canada is establishing a Grasslands National Park in southwest Saskatchewan. It will consist of two vast blocks of land, both located adjacent to possible Buffalo Commons counties across the border in Montana—eventually three hundred square miles in all, possibly to be stocked with herds of buffalo.

"How did the ranchers take it?" I inquire. Government buyouts lie behind much of the project's land acquisitions.

"That's the weird part," Frank says. "They were all for it; couldn't sell out fast enough. A lot of the Canadian ranchers are mad at the government, but mostly because they think setting up the park took too long. They say it should have been installed ten years ago, when they were all young enough to take the money and head for some nice warm climate."

Late in April *USA Today's* weekend edition sponsors a nation-wide phone-in poll in its 340 newspapers. The subject is "Are Ranchers Killing the West?" Any reader with a touch-tone phone may register an opinion. The choices are one sentence long:

1. Should ranchers let cattle continue to graze on public lands?
2. Should we kick cattle off and establish a Buffalo Commons for wildlife throughout the West?
3. Should ranchers and environmentalists compromise?

Frank and Deborah Popper, sitting over Sunday-morning coffee at their dining room table in Highland Park, are taken aback to open the New Brunswick paper, the *Home News*, and see this exercise in land-use opinion-polling.

"They've got the Buffalo Commons in the wrong place," moans Deborah.

Frank is not listening. Over Deborah's protests he is headed for their touch-tone kitchen phone, eyes bright, Sunday supplement in hand.

In the end, they both call in.

"Push two for the Buffalo Commons," says the calm recorded voice, and Frank does. He claims it is his duty as a scholar and a patriot and a Chicagoan to vote early and often, but Deborah will not let him. Deborah pushes three, for compromise. When the results come out three weeks later, it doesn't matter much: of 12,340 votes cast, 65 percent of the respondents are in favor of continued cattle grazing, 7 percent want to see environmentalists and ranchers work together, and 28 percent vote for a Buffalo Commons.

Deborah is depressed by the lack of interest in compromise.

Frank is more sanguine. When I arrive at Lucy Stone Hall the next day to read the latest buffalo mail, he is leaning back in his swivel chair, gazing out the window at a brilliant early-summer afternoon, studying the fanning, swaying boughs of the white pine that grows just beyond his office wall. Singly and in clusters a great many of its long graceful needles are turning yellow, or brown, or a bleached gray-white. On the Plains you might suspect the evergreen of falling victim to drought, but the New Jersey spring has been wetter than usual. Too wet; the tree is suffering from acid rain.

Frank Popper is still thinking about the USA *Today* poll.

"Less than four years ago," he says, "the Buffalo Commons concept didn't even exist. Now the idea and much of what it stands for have entered the American language, wild and free. At this rate a Commons will happen faster than we ever antici-pated. Our name doesn't even need to be attached. Not bad. Not bad at all."

He hands me a fistful of new mail and turns back to his desk, taking another gulp of cold coffee from his buffalo mug. The last term papers for his Environmental Policy course need to be marked and the grade sheets sent off to the Rutgers registrar before nightfall. A corrected manuscript on the future of Ameri-can regional planning must be mailed to the editor of a scholarly review up at MIT.

The envelopes Frank has handed me are all addressed in large, careful cursive writing. The Poppers and the Buffalo Commons have just been featured in a children's environmen-tal magazine, and dozens of letters are coming in. I scan the batch in my hand; the return addresses include elementary schools in Rhode Island, Wyoming, Texas, Michigan, Ala-bama, Oregon, Delaware, Tennessee.

From Cheyenne Kills Right, age twelve, of Brooklyn, New York:

Dear Frank and Deborah Popper,
My father is Sioux Indian. My ancestors hunted buffalo. I told my aunt about you guys believing in prairies and sharing the land with the buffalo. She lives in South Dakota. She likes the idea a lot. Keep up the good work all the way!

From Cortney Johnson, age ten, Alamo, North Dakota:

Dear Mr. and Mrs. Popper,
If you think the government should turn a state into a buffalo reserve then turn your state into one!

Neither missive persuades me that the American argument on the fate of the Plains will be finished any time soon. Across the crowded office Frank Popper scribbles a hasty reminder to himself, dropping it conspicuously atop his attaché case to avoid last-minute forgetfulness. He needs to stop on the way home at the travel agency in the New Brunswick mall, to pick up the two ultra-supersaver tickets that are waiting there.

In the morning he and Deborah have a flight to catch. Out on the flat, dry plains of eastern Wyoming, a television crew from the Canadian Broadcasting System is shooting a documentary series on North America's plains; the Poppers will watch some of the filming, then talk on camera about the returning frontier.

Then the Poppers are heading even deeper into the Plains. They are scheduled to talk all across Wyoming and Colorado on the Buffalo Commons, lecturing at three state campuses and at citizen forums in three small farming towns.

"The Commons is at heart a metaphor," Deborah plans to insist at every stop. "*Metaphor.* A new way of reading the land." She pauses. "Buffalo are lovely, especially roaming on the Plains. I just never thought so many people would agree. Or care so much. Is it our fault, that an idea happened to match the times?"

As scholarly terrain and as American landscape the Great Plains are only flat and peaceful at first look. Just four years ago the Poppers roamed a conspicuously silent West, one fenced about with historical taboos as strong as barbed wire. Now the Poppers are heading into a flyover country alive with argument, anger, and painful reflection. Since they wrote their original article on the Plains' dismal outlook in 1987, Frank and Deborah Popper have seen much of their academic prophecy turn to fact: the S & L crises, the ongoing Plains droughts, the increased credibility of the greenhouse effect, the shift in U.S.–Russian relations, the rise in environmental conscience.

Across the Great Plains, four years after the Poppers became the region's best source of conversation since Custer, twelve decades of depopulation and divided loyalties are bringing, at last, an unexpected harvest. Through all its hard history the twin luxuries of choice and doubt have been as rare as rainfall beyond the 98th meridian. The Poppers' vision of the American prairie restored, buffalo and all, may be poetry or possibility, but the power of their idea to thrill and to outrage has begun to make the Plains states think, as well as react; plan, as well as endure.

Other conversations across time concerning the West and its future are also accelerating: Patricia Nelson Limerick and Frederick Jackson Turner, Wes Jackson and Walter Prescott Webb; Vine Deloria, Jr., and Bret Wallach; the patriotic booster Gilpin and the visionary patriot John Wesley Powell. The Poppers, as usual, talk to anyone.

But to the question that awakens them in the middle of the New Jersey night—"What have we done to the Plains?"—neither Popper has a completely satisfying reply.

"How much we have changed the equation is hard to tell," Deborah insists. "It's scary," says Frank, gazing at a clipping from the *Denver Post*, "to think we might have had something to do with stuff like *this*."

A band of Lakota Sioux, the Denver paper reports, has announced that they are laying claim, as of the summer of 1991, to the western half of South Dakota (including Ellsworth Air Force Base, 150 Minuteman missile silos, and the Homestake Gold Mine). Non-Indians living within the new Lakota homeland, the declaration says, will be allowed to remain as foreign nationals. A return to a buffalo-based economy is envisioned by the year 2016.

After their latest Western speaking tour, the Poppers can count on nearly a month of high summer to roam the Plains before the Rutgers school year closes in again, and with it the exams to devise, and the statistics to review, and the land-use journals to read, and the phone calls to return.

Every hour out of New Brunswick seems precious, and Deborah and Frank are full of ideas. They want to visit with wheat farmers and government climatologists, small-town business people and water-rights brokers. To examine the black-footed ferret reintroduction project in Sybille, Wyoming. To drive across a hundred miles of former shortgrass prairie in the eastern part of that state, once overgrazed, then overplowed, now deserted. Maybe investigate some distressed counties, maybe visit Colorado's Pawnee National Grassland, or swing up to Custer State Park in western South Dakota to admire the buffalo herds.

But it is a long way yet from here to there. For now the Poppers will edit each other's speeches on the plane to Cheyenne, talking their way west, toughing it out.

Afterword

By the autumn of 1992 the Buffalo Commons debate has acquired even more complications. State and federal response to the Commons idea is still part torpor, part distaste, part reluctantly increasing attention. But the Nature Conservancy and other private preservation groups, after years of neglecting the Plains, have begun major buy-ups in or near the region, with plans to restock buffalo and other native wildlife on the newly purchased lands.

From Montana to Texas, Plains landowners (farmers and ranchers both) have begun returning enormous acreage to game habitat—which is then leased, at handsome rates, to urban hunters. My cousin and her physician husband left their city jobs in Aberdeen last year and bought 3,500 acres in South Dakota's rolling Big Bend country, along the Missouri River. Their new property is only a mile or so west of the prairie lands our great-grandfather Matthews struggled to turn from shortgrass to wheat farm in the 1890s. Hunters fly in from across the country now to shoot Canada geese, ringneck pheasant, duck, grouse. ("We also book buffalo hunts," states the four-color brochure for Big Bend Ranch, with modest pride.)

In the deep rural Plains, to the Poppers' delighted surprise, a multitude of local, for-profit variations on the Commons are suddenly turning up. Ranchers in the Northern Plains are starting to run buffalo in record numbers; some herds are now eight thousand, even ten thousand strong. ("Hey, it's a growth sector," one rancher whispered to the Poppers, after a particularly bile-laden Commons forum in backcountry Wyoming.) Recruits to buffaloism range from Ted Turner to Sam Hurst, the NBC producer from Los Angeles who followed the Poppers through Oklahoma for the "Today Show." He quit his job early in 1992 and moved his family to western South Dakota. He's a buffalo rancher now, and says his memories of Burbank are fading fast, especially in calving season.

Twenty-nine Indian tribes, up from just six in 1991, are back in the buffalo business. The Native American Fish and Wildlife Society, headquartered in Colorado, has launched a consortium of Western tribes in large-scale buffalo-herd management. Several Montana tribes are negotiating—suing, actually—for the right to claim buffalo that wander out of Yellowstone and onto state land. U.S. and Canadian Sioux are attempting an international confederacy to create a tribal herd. Curing the economic, social, and spiritual impoverishment of the Plains, all say, cannot be done without reintroducing buffalo and the buffalo culture.

"We want the region to be more self-sufficient, after all," a Sioux leader from South Dakota informed the Poppers at a symposium in the winter of 1991, "and the buffalo clearly belong here." Frank and Deborah nodded gravely.

Shortly after that, Frank Popper called me. "Guess what?" he demanded. "The Buffalo Commons was invented long before Deborah and me. George Catlin thought it up in 1841. Of course, nobody listened to him, either. Thank God for tenure."

George Catlin's hundreds of detailed oil sketches and letters, produced during his journeys on the Plains between 1832 and 1839, form the only complete record of Plains Indian culture at its height. His paintings preserve tribal ceremonials and buffalo chases, family meals and children's games. His writings testify to the richness of Plains animal life and foretell, with despairing accuracy, the changes that white settlement will bring to the American prairies. To save even a portion of the world he saw vanishing all about him, Catlin envisioned the creation of an enormous reserve for Indians and buffalo.

"In future what a splendid contemplation," he wrote, ". . . when one imagines them as they *might* be seen, by some great protecting policy of government preserved in their beauty and wildness, in a *magnificent park*, where the world could see for ages to come . . . the fleeting herds of elks and buffaloes . . . A *Nation's Park*, containing man and beast, in all the freshness of their nature's beauty."

The Smithsonian's 1852 attempt to provide a permanent home for Catlin's paintings of Plains life was voted down by Congress. In 1872, impoverished and forgotten, Catlin died in Jersey City, New Jersey, an inlet and a headland away from the stretch of grasslands road where Frank and Deborah Popper would one day sit in traffic and argue the fate of the Plains.

—October 1992